Dome Builder's Handbook No.2

William Yarnall

With a Directory of Manufacturers
by Andrew Ralph and William Yarnall

Running Press
Philadelphia, Pennsylvania

Canadian representatives: John Wiley & Sons Canada, Ltd.
22 Worcester Road, Rexdale, Ontario M9W 1L1

International representatives: Kaiman & Polon, Inc.
2175 Lemoine Avenue, Fort Lee, New Jersey 07024

9 8 7 6 5 4 3 2 1
Digit on the right indicates the number of this printing.

Library of Congress Cataloging in Publication Data

Yarnall, William, 1951–
  Dome Builder's Handbook No. 2
  Bibliography: p.
  1. Geodesic domes—Design and construction. I. Title.
TH2170.Y37   690'.8   78-15533
ISBN 0-89471-043-5 library binding
ISBN 0-89471-042-7 paperback

Cover illustration: Seymour Chwast
Cover design and interior design: James Wizard Wilson
Editor: Alida Becker

Typography: Oracle, by Comp•Art, Philadelphia, Pennsylvania
Color photos printed by Pearl Pressman Liberty, Philadelphia, Pennsylvania
Printed and bound by Port City Press, Baltimore, Maryland

This book may be ordered directly from the publisher.
Please include 25 cents postage.
Try your bookstore first.
Running Press
38 South Nineteenth Street
Philadelphia, Pennsylvania 19103

Acknowledgments

Without the help of the following people, *Dome Builder's Handbook No. 2* would not have been possible:

Andrew Ralph compiled the list of dome manufacturers, wrote detailed descriptions of their products and services, and analyzed the quality and cost of their domes. His professional experience and his common sense put this section of the book on a sure footing.

Howard Johnson gave freely of his time and talents, providing valuable advice on building techniques and planning. His architectural drawings were an added bonus.

Mercy Johnson supplied many photographs to illustrate important phases of the building process.

Ken Kern was kind enough to allow us to reprint his home builders' test.

Carey Smoot furnished architectural drawings and all the color photographs. Throughout the writing of the book, he made himself available to answer questions and offered many helpful suggestions. His eye for detail, his insight, and his expertise added immeasurably to the project.

Photographs

PAGE

iii	Monterey Domes
v	Expodome International Ltd.
viii	Monterey Domes
9	Nancy Martin
10	Rowland Mainstone
13	Space Structures International
14	Public Relations Department, City of Montreal
15, 17	Nancy Martin
18	Public Relations Department, City of Montreal
19	The Big Outdoors People/William Whittenberg
30	Domes and Homes Inc.
31	The Big Outdoors People/William Whittenberg
32	Expodome International Ltd.
49–64	Color photographs by Carey Smoot
65–71	Mercy Johnson
74, 75	Cathedralite Domes
76–87	Mercy Johnson
88	Cathedralite Domes
89	Domes Geodyssey
91	Monterey Domes
92–94	The Big Outdoors People/William Whittenberg
95	Cathedralite Domes
96	Domes & Homes
	Domes Geodyssey/Smith Productions
	Domes Geodyssey/DHS Inc.
97	Dyna Dome
98	Expodome International Ltd.
99	Geodesic Domes Inc.
	Geodesic Homes
100	The Hasey Company

PAGE

100	The Hasey Company
	Hexadome Inc.
101	Hexadome Inc.
	Monterey Domes
	Monterey Domes
102	Monterey Domes
	Shelter Construction and Development Ltd.
	Shelter Construction and Development Ltd./J. Jenkins
103	Space Structures International
104	Synapse/Scott Sims
105	Tension Structures, Inc.
106	Western Hemisphere Ltd.
108	Spirex Structures Inc.
109	Spirex Structures Inc.
	Temcor
	Temcor
110	Triodetic Structures Ltd.
	Triodetic Structures Ltd.
	Triodetic Structures Ltd.
	Unadilla Silo Company, Inc.
111	Unadilla Silo Company, Inc.
112	Space Structures International
113	Fabrico Manufacturing Corporation
114	Dyna Dome
115	John Martin
116–118	Carey Smoot
119	Leland Lee
120, 121	Carey Smoot
122	Dome West
126	Synapse/Scott Sims

CONTENTS

Chapter 1.   A Brief Look at the Dome   9
    The First Domes
    Astronomy and Domes
    The Way Domes Work
    Buckminster Fuller and the Popularity of Domes
    The Role of the Dome

Chapter 2.   Are You a Potential Dome Home Owner?   19
    Some Things to Remember About Domes
    Other Uses for Domes
    Building Codes and Permits
    Architectural Boards and Committees
    Organizing to Change Building and Zoning Regulations
    Building Yourself or Contracting
    Ken Kerns' Home Builders' Test
    Manufacturers, Contractors, and Contracts
    Inspections

    Architectural plans following page 32
    Color photos following page 48

Chapter 3.   Property and Materials   65
    Choosing Your Property
    Site Considerations
    Foundations
    The Two Main Kinds of Domes
    Windows
    Materials

Chapter 4.   Some Basics of Dome Building   77
    Foundations
    Strut, Skin, and Panel Construction
    Shingling

Chapter 5.   Dome Manufacturers   89
    Commercial Dome Home Manufacturers
    Dome Building Consultants
    Industrial and Commercial Manufacturers

Chapter 6.   Custom Dome Building   115

Bibliography   123

Chapter 1. A Brief Look at the Dome

THE FIRST DOMES

Throughout what is known as the civilized world, the most common shape for houses is a straight-sided square or rectangle. The evolutionary process that brought this shape into such overwhelming domination has been going on since the first human being sought shelter from the forces of nature.

Our attitudes towards ourselves, our environment, and our heritage are reflected in our dwellings—and these have undergone many changes. And if a home tells a lot about its occupants, what do today's designs reflect? What should we think about when we start planning a home?

How about going back to the very beginning, when our distant ancestors had an almost reverent feeling about the places where they lived, back to the very origins of history, to man's initial attempts to protect himself from the elements, and to the dome—the shape of his first dwellings.

In the beginning, everyone built their own homes with their own hands, and obviously the finished product was something deeply personal. Home was a lot more than a place to hang your hat. It was the most important place in a person's life, a symbol of his ties to his family, his ancestors, even to the cosmic order.

Primitive people solved some complex problems in meeting their immediate needs, and they also developed a deep spiritual bond with their dwellings. Their homes were built with whatever was immediately at hand: for the framework, they used pliable materials like branches, saplings, thatching, and animal skins; the shape was usually more or less circular. This meant that some kind of curved roof was needed—and herein lies the origin of the dome.

As generations passed, the dome became an important architectural form. With more sophisticated tools and building methods, straighter lines replaced circular ones, but in spite of this the dome was preserved because of its symbolic significance.

From its beginning, the dome was linked with boats and shipbuilding techniques because of the obvious similarities in design. The first shelters were made of saplings and thatch; the first seagoing vessels were made of reeds, descendants of the reed basket. These reed basket boats could even be turned upside down and used as shelters.

Aside from their structural similarities, the natural laws observed by shipbuilders could also be related to domes. For example, consider the mast and boom of a ship: because the mast is vertical, the gravitational force exerted on it is focused at one particular point; with the boom, however, the force of gravity is spread along the entire horizontal length of the pole. Horizontal and vertical elements both have inherent strengths and weaknesses, but when they're integrated in the dome, the weaknesses are minimized.

The first step in transforming the early dome into something more permanent than reed and thatch came with the use of heavier wooden materials. With more experience and better tools, builders could produce wooden domes on a monumental scale. These domes were free-standing, and their walls were relatively light. After they were fully raised and protected from the elements, wooden domes were sometimes decorated—even completely covered with a gilded metal sheathing. These larger structures became granaries, tombs, and baths. But since wood can be worked with relative ease, this, combined with its advantages as a building material, led to its excessive use and depletion in many areas.

As society gradually became more organized and cultures became more refined and stable, there began to be a need to preserve ancestral buildings and make them more permanent. Stone was the first of these more permanent materials. It was being widely used for dome building as early as the middle of the second millenium B.C. By 1300 B.C. the art of building with stone had vastly matured, as shown by the famous Tomb of Atreus, a magnificent Greek building which has a diameter of 48½ feet at its base.

The early stone domes were all what are called "false" domes. This refers to the way they were built, which gave them more of a conical look when they were completed. An initial ring of stones served as a foundation, then other rings were added until the top was capped by a single stone, always larger than the others. The shape was achieved by bedding each ring further inward—it wasn't necessary to lay each course further back upon the course below because of the horizontal force achieved through jamming the rocks tightly together to complete each successive ring. Although this made the dome stable when each course was finished, the same force sometimes caused the stones to slip against one

another. To prevent this, larger, heavier stones were used.

Knowledge of the great outward thrust inherent in stone domes was undoubtedly gained at the cost of lives. After many early stone domes collapsed, support was added by bracing them on the outside. Rammed earth was one way of doing this—huge mounds of dirt were piled around the entire dome, holding the blocks together while allowing them to settle against one another. This was the method used in the Tomb of Atreus, which is still standing today. The entire tomb was covered by a mountain of earth. Not only did it remain hidden, but it could be destroyed only from within, a risky venture at best. Later, when durable anchor chain was developed, huge links were strung like giant girdles around the Romans' massive domes, completely enclosing them.

Some early brick domes were constructed in a slightly different way than the stone domes, and these are the forerunners of what is called the "true" dome, in which the backs of the blocks were tilted slightly upward at the same time that they were projected inward. Both brick and stone domes were built without precise measuring devices, and it was possible to learn a great deal by experimenting. Dome roofs were even built on rectangular shelters by projecting corner bricks further inward than others on the initial rings. Eventually, a circular shape was achieved, and from that the dome was completed.

The Romans used concrete to cast huge domes over their baths and public houses. This building material went through various stages of development. At first the brickwork contained as much brick as it did mortar, but it developed in quality with the discovery of better mortar, a clay from the Bay of Naples. Eventually the Romans were able to dispense with permanent facings for their walls and only needed timber to support their foundations and vaults. When they had hardened sufficiently, these concrete masses were capable of standing on their own. One of the finest is the dome of Hadrian's Pantheon, completed about 128 A.D. It has a diameter of 43.3 meters (about 142 feet) and was unequalled until the Renaissance.

The Roman Pantheon has a circular base which is thicker and heavier than the upper part of the dome. Although the lower portions give it added strength, the dome was hollowed out inside at regular intervals to reduce what was felt to be excessive weight.

The Tomb of Klytemnestra.

In the higher parts of the dome the concrete is thinner, so its total weight is lighter, a protection against outward thrust. The concrete itself is also a lighter variety. The very top of the Pantheon is open, another means of reducing the total weight. This hole, called the "eye," is strengthened by a solid ring of brickwork.

Concrete was an important development in the evolution of architecture and building materials. Working with concrete doesn't involve the time, effort, and skills needed for stonecutting, and concrete structures often last longer than those made with separate pieces of stone. With the use of concrete, building also became more complex, and intricate buttressing systems had to be devised. In some designs involving more than one dome, the walls of one were often used to support the others. This was done so well that an untrained eye might not even notice the buttressing effect. In the Pantheon, virtually every form of buttressing known to the Romans was used.

ASTRONOMY AND DOMES

The Greek and Romans' wide knowledge of mathematics and geometry probably accounts for the precision with which they designed their buildings. Plato was familiar with the five ways in which a sphere can be divided with total regularity, and it has been suggested that even before his time navigators from the Near East had already sailed completely around the globe, secure in the knowledge that the earth was indeed round. Astronomy was on its way to becoming an exacting science. Considering the primitive thatched dome huts of antiquity and the cosmic symbolism they had for their inhabitants, it's ironic that the study of astronomy led to the modern world's first geodesic dome, a planetarium.

The planetarium went through various stages of development, as did astronomy. Early man believed that the earth was supported by a god. A marble carving found in Italy, dated at around 73 B.C. and thought by some archaeologists to be much older, depicts the world—represented as a sphere—supported on the shoulders of Atlas. Called the Farnese Globe, it is made of white marble and is one of the earliest celestial globes. On it are carved many of the constellations we know today, and the movements of the sun are represented by parallel lines.

The armillary sphere, an offspring of the celestial globe, represents the solar system in skeletal form. Armillary spheres are a framework of rings which represent astronomical circles, the horizon, and the path of the sun. Although their scientific value is highly questionable, they're certainly beautiful works of art. The first important armillary sphere was the Gottorb Globe built by Andreas Busch around 1657 under the direction of Adam Oelschlager, a librarian and court mathematician of Frederick III. The globe was about 11 feet in diameter and mechanized so that within its brass meridian circle it made one revolution every 24 hours. The part of the framework representing the equator was made to rotate once in 25,000 years, the rate of the precessional motion of the earth. A brass ball represented the sun, and six silver angels symbolized the known planets and their orbits. The outer rings of this sphere showed the constellations in bronze figures and the brighter stars in silver. The Gottorb Globe could be entered through a door and held up to twelve people at a time. It was lighted by two small lamps, driven by water power, and weighed about three and a half tons. It's interesting to note that the earth was shown as the third planet from the sun, a fact that was still questionable at the time.

A major problem in the development of planetaria was the accurate depiction of stellar movements as observed from within a structure. Since the heavens seemed to move about our "fixed" position, it was only logical that the first planetaria were designed to move. Gear trains were designed through computation to impart the correct relative motion of the planets. One such globe, called the "Astronomical Machine," was built in 1758. It had an eighteen-foot diameter and could hold about thirty people inside. Holes punctured in the shell represented stars. It was lit from the outside, and each star had its appropriate relative brightness. In 1911 Dr. Wallace Atwood designed a similar globe which was fifteen feet in diameter and driven by electricity. Though the "Astronomical Machine" was destroyed 120 years after its completion, the globe designed by Dr. Atwood is still in existence.

Although these globes were functional, there was an inherent conceptual drawback—accommodations were limited. Just a handful of people could use the facilities at one time. The problem of designing a large yet accurate sphere was brought to the Zeiss optical firm of Germany in 1913. For six years, they were unable to find a solution until Dr. Walter Baversfeld thought of reversing the mechanical process.

Instead of mechanizing the sphere, Baversfeld decided to mechanize the optical projectors and reproduce the celestial images on a hemisphere much larger than the original sphere. This, the first geodesic dome, was a highly subdivided icosahedron constructed with a framework of light iron rods accurate in length to two-thousandths of an inch. Great circle arches were used as supportive structural members. Very thin cement covered the outside of the dome; the inside was lined with wood, curved just enough to facilitate the application of thin layers of cement. The ratio of the shell's thickness to the diameter of the dome was based on that between an eggshell and an egg.

Thus the world saw not only its first geodesic dome but its first lightweight, thin-shell, concrete dome. The planetarium was awesome, amazing to even the men who designed it. It was highly publicized, and shortly thereafter representatives from other cities became interested in planetaria. This led to the further development of the dome in Europe.

THE WAY DOMES WORK

In working with domes and understanding why they have such great durability and strength, it's important to know a little bit about their basics. The most important element in any geodesic dome is the triangle—the polyhedral faces of every dome can be divided into triangles. As a matter of fact, the triangle is basic for all forms of structural stability since it's the only construction that's truly rigid. Let's use an example of two boards nailed together. They're certainly not rigid, and even if two more boards are connected to create a square, this assemblage is no more rigid than the first. In fact, no number of boards nailed together in this way will become rigid until a method of triangulation is introduced. Even though it's not always visible, the triangle is involved in all structures.

In creating the framework for a dome, what is actually constructed is a complex network of triangles that roughly approximates a sphere—the more complex the network of triangles, the more nearly the structure resembles a sphere. Forming triangles of various sizes, a sphere can be divided symetrically by thirty-one great circles. Great circles are the largest possible circles that can be drawn upon the surface of a sphere; because they are all maximum bands of length, stress applied at any particular point is shifted and passed throughout the entire band. Every great circle cuts a sphere exactly in half, so the term used by mathematicians to describe these curves is geodesic, which comes from the Greek for "earth dividing." The word was originally used in connection with surveys of such large areas of land that the curvature of the earth had to be included in the calculations.

Consider the icosahedron, a twenty-sided polyhedron that can be divided up into a network of triangular faces. Each face of the icosa can be further subdivided, and there's more than one way of accomplishing this. The number of divisions made in each icosa face is referred to as its frequency, represented by the symbol "v." The higher the frequency, the greater the number of triangles, and with this complexity the shape becomes more spherical. Each triangle in the sphere shifts whatever stress is applied to it equilaterally throughout the other triangles. The greater the number of subdivisions, the greater the distribution of stress—and the stronger and more efficient the structure becomes. In other words, each member supports the others in an interlocking system. Taking this into consideration, stress analysis used in conventional building has no bearing on the strength of geodesic domes because it deals with applied stress to a particular part of the whole.

Because the geometry applied in dome construction is so precise, there are other benefits inherent in the structure. It is the most efficient process of enclosing space, encompassing the maximum area with the minimum amount of materials. It's relatively easy to heat and cool, and conserves both because it exposes the least possible amount of surface to the elements. Many parts of the geodesic dome are identical, so it's suitable for mass production. Also, because so many parts are repeated, construction becomes relatively easy as long as the measurements are careful and precise.

BUCKMINSTER FULLER AND THE POPULARITY OF DOMES

The one name most commonly associated with the geodesic dome is, of course, R. Buckminster Fuller. It was largely through his efforts that the dome achieved such popularity. But if it hadn't been for his dynamic personal appeal—and the fact that his patents were so meticulous no corporate conglomerate could find a way around them—his name might not be as well known as it is today.

Fuller's geodesic dome and his many other contributions to housing design all stem from a highly idealized, humanitarian philosophy and his insights into the nature of the universe. Hearing a Buckminster Fuller discourse on the universe, nature, and the ultimate interrelatedness of things, one can easily fall into the trap of classifying him with seers, mystics, and unfathomable foggy prophets. Perhaps too much has been forgotten. There was the Bucky Fuller who didn't graduate from col-

Buckminster Fuller's dome at Montreal Expo, 1968.

lege (his degrees are all honorary), carried meat for the American Meat Company, and served in the navy during World War I; a Bucky Fuller who lived beyond his means, slept on the floor, met all kinds of people from Eugene O'Neil to Al Capone, and even contemplated suicide by the banks of Lake Michigan. Despite his genius, life dealt him periods of crushing depression, self-doubt, and financial difficulty.

But it was at this low ebb of his life, when most people would focus simply on self-preservation, that Fuller resolved to use his talents to serve humanity. Making a living was just something that interfered with his larger endeavors. In his view, the new technology and its rapidly advancing industrialization were completely misunderstood, and man's attempts to exploit them prevented their natural evolution. Since man's environment plays a large role in the development of human nature, which again in turn affects man's environment, Fuller decided to improve upon our environment.

This led him to design a house on a pole that would weigh 6,000 pounds and could be mass-produced to sell for $1,500. Basically it was a hexagon supported by a strong central column, braced with cable and compression struts. Beneath the house, there was space for a car, plus a jet-propelled wingless aircraft. Like a lot of other Buckminster Fuller designs, it was a bit ahead of its time, especially for 1927. Originally called the 4D house—a reference to time, Einstein's fourth dimension—the name was changed after Fuller's conversation with a public relations man who observed his frequent use of the words, "dynamic," "maximum," and "ion." Thus, the dymaxion house. Numerous inventions followed, the dymaxion car and the dymaxion bathroom truck among others.

Fuller was concerned with the betterment of man's environment, but unfortunately the implementation of his designs also necessitated a close relationship with the industrial world, big business, and the big money mentality usually associated with

14

financial enterprise. Fuller was suspicious of these groups, and had his problems.

A design he had developed for a dymaxion car was taken over by the Kaiser laboratories, who left Fuller out in the dark. Much later, he received a letter from Henry Kaiser informing him that the project had been abandoned. Fuller's lightweight engine had been replaced by one weighing hundreds of pounds; everything was thrown out of balance, so of course the car didn't work. In fact, it smashed into a tree. Since Fuller's name and trademark had been used, his reputation was tarnished.

The Dymaxion Dwelling Machine, a refinement of Fuller's 4D house, led to the formation of Fuller Houses Inc., another enterprise that was killed by commercial exploitation. After World War II there was a need for housing and a need to provide work for thousands of skilled laborers who were flooding the market. The commercial development and production of the 4D house would meet both needs, but Fuller realized that before this could happen time and money had to be put into his venture. He set 1952 as a target date for completion, got a contract from the government for two prototypes, and began work.

The new Dymaxion Dwelling Machine was a vast improvement over the old 4D. It was perfectly round, 118 feet in circumference instead of the old hexagonal shape. The walls were sheet aluminum, and the windows were formed by a band of tinted plexiglass. The ceiling was a sixteen-foot dome topped by a ventilator designed to provide natural air conditioning.

The Dymaxion Dwelling Machine was put on public exhibition in 1945, gained widespread attention, and was greeted enthusiastically by the public. Orders poured in. Despite the fact that Fuller's structure was only a prototype, he could have sold out for a profit of at least half a million dollars. But the whole scheme was repulsive to him. Although the military could handle production of the design, he knew it wasn't ready for the public. He never developed a final plan, all his backers sold out, the business was shut down, and no one made any money.

After this fiasco, Fuller turned his complete attention to the mastery of spherical trigonometry. He was intrigued by the dome forms found in nature. It's been said that the designs he produced are actually just huge diagrams of the natural fields of atomic force that hold all matter together.

By rotating the icosahedron in every way possible, Fuller came up with the pattern of the thirty-one great circles. But here he made a decision that influenced the design of all his future domes—he chose not to use the great circles as explicit structural members, removing them, in effect, to the realm of pure principle. The resulting structure maintained the interplay between tension and compression within highly subdivided faces of the icosahedron; great circles and portions of great circles were not specifically designed to play a role as supporting structural members. This was the basis for Fuller's patent for a space-enclosing structure, applied for in December 1951 and granted in June 1954.

As domes became popular among industrial builders, this patent protected Fuller and brought his name into the limelight. In 1953, at the age of 58, he got his first big break. The Ford Motor Company wanted a dome to cover the rotunda of their River Rouge plant, but the engineers calculated that the structure would have to weigh at least 160 tons, which would collapse the entire building. Henry Ford II decided to call in Buckminster Fuller for the job. Fuller designed a dome that would weigh eight and a half tons, and was awarded the contract. The project was to be completed in four months, and Fuller finished it two days ahead of schedule.

The Ford dome was built with the octet truss construction method, requiring 19,680 one-yard struts weighing five ounces each. The octet trusses were riveted together to form the triangular and tetrahedral parts of the dome; the holes at the ends of the struts were spaced within a tolerance of five-thousandths of an inch.

After this project, interest in domes soared, and the dome business grew along with it. The government was setting up the D.E.W. line, a radar system to provide early warning in the event of nuclear attack; when they approached Fuller he designed a system of domes that was later built by General Electric. And this was just the beginning. Big industry wanted domes, universities wanted domes, even children wanted play domes—and they were built with everything from plywood to plastic to card-

15

board.

But even today Fuller's plans for the dome go far beyond all this. His mind works on a monumental scale— the future of humanity and its environment. His visions of domed-over cities and floating spheres are eye-openers. Consider a city covered by a futuristic dome with structural members so delicate, and the dome itself so high, that it would be barely noticeable. It would be possible to regulate sunlight; in fact, all weather conditions within the dome would be under control.

Fuller feels that this type of stabilized environment would give man an increasing sense of mobility, a sense that could be carried even further in floating geodesic spheres encompassing whole cities. The number of uses for geodesic domes seems as limitless as the imagination—industrial domes, domed cities, and floating spherical islands. A new geodesic planet seems entirely conceivable.

But what about the smaller, more personal levels of dome construction? What about the individual family home and Fuller's dream of a low-cost, mass-produced dwelling designed to upgrade everyone's environment? A radical change on an individual level is difficult, exciting, and challenging. But most people who consider building a home are not thinking on the philosophical level, or even on the level of universal practicality—they're concerned about their own personal needs.

Fuller's plywood dome homes did not catch on, either philosophically or practically. However, a link *did* develop between Fuller's overall concept, the obvious attractions of the dome as an alternate environment, and a youthful, idealistic trend toward improving both personal and universal space. The dome caught on not only because it was practical but also because its structure came to represent a progressive group of people.

Dome building turned into a phenomenon. Fuller already had a well-established and well-deserved reputation. His numerous speaking engagements produced more and more publicity. All sorts of things became associated with Fuller's views. Suddenly his deepest insights and his highly ordered world of precision were swept up by the counterculture, and Fuller became a cult hero. His commitment to the improvement of the human environment was reduced to one highly publicized, displaced obsession—domes.

Members of the counterculture were the first to adopt the geodesic dome as a living space. They were in the news and so were the domes they built. Domes have a futuristic, progressive look and, as photographers soon realized, they're aesthetically appealing and intriguing. But these domes were not Fuller's idea of a precisely designed, mass-produced product capable of being shipped and assembled anywhere. They were all handcrafted, built with collective know-how and whatever materials were locally available.

These domes symbolized their builders' hopes for the beginning of a new kind of civilization. One group of architectural students and artists who attended a Fuller lecture at Boulder, Colorado, were inspired to build a communal settlement using domes. Drop City, the first geodesic community, was founded on the outskirts of Trinidad, Colorado. It was more than a community of new structures, it was an experiment in living. People were free to come and go as they pleased, and Drop City became a stopover on the route to the West Coast during the Haight Ashbury days.

The first dome at Drop City was an eighteen-foot-diameter dodecahedron built from plywood and 2 X 4's. It was covered with tarpaper fastened to chicken wire with bottlecaps and stucco, and waterproofed with tar. The whole thing was finished with a fibered aluminum coat. Glass from old cars was used for the windows and 2 X 4's were laid down for the floor—whatever happened to be handy. Later, some domes at Drop City were made from car tops. Others became very complex, including a fused, triple rhombicosadodecahedron—or zome—based on a design by Steve Baer. The community itself functioned on a leisurely basis, and everyone did pretty much what they wanted, when they wanted. There were no strict rules. Today, more than a decade later, Drop City is deserted.

After Drop City was begun, dome structures began to pop up with greater and greater frequency, usually the handiwork of enthusiastic young builders. A lot of this activity took place in the Southwest, where population was less dense and there were few building restrictions. When there *were* building code violations, there was usually no one around to interfere, and building inspectors often could do nothing about an already completed dome.

By this time, the dome had been removed from its place within Buckminster Fuller's carefully planned world. Its natural appeal and the growing demand for more creativity and variation in structural design combined to create a dome boom. The prime movers behind this were the "sun dome," which was introduced in the May 1966 issue of *Popular Science,* and *Domebooks 1* and *2,* which first appeared in 1970 and 1971.

Popular Science's sun dome was a backyard project made of thin sticks and covered with plastic film. For five dollars, customers could buy plans for 16½- and 30-foot-diameter domes, building instructions, and a license from Buckminster Fuller to construct one dome. These structures could be used as covers for swimming pools, outdoor playhouses, screened gazebos, and greenhouses. They had several appealing qualities: the solar heat they provided allowed pools to be used for a longer period of time, the plastic skins could easily be replaced with screens, the cost was extraordinarily modest, and construction was simple. The whole thing could be assembled or dismantled within a couple of hours, and three people could easily lift the structure even when it was entirely assembled.

Domebooks 1 and *2,* put together by a group led by Lloyd Kahn, contained valuable basic information and guidelines for do-it-yourself construction. Enthusiasm seemed to have reached its height when *Popular Science* referred to Kahn as the "Pied Piper of Domedom." But slowly, for various structural and ecological reasons, Kahn became disenchanted with domes and allowed *Domebooks 1* and *2* to go out of print. *Domebook 3* was incorporated into *Shelter,* a colossal collection of handbuilt dwellings from all over the world.

The domes described in *Domebook 2* were never intended as permanent middle-class housing, but many of its readers were attracted by the low building costs (about a thousand dollars) and were anxious to employ their own talents in creating houses. A lot of them found that dome building was far from easy. In fact, one of Kahn's own criticisms of *Domebook 2* was that it made building and maintaining a dome look too simple. It was *Domebook 2,* however, that publicized the math, materials, and plans necessary to make amateur dome building a reality.

By 1972, the dome home had really come into its own. Its elegance, potential, and desirability had spread far beyond the counterculture and blossomed through all levels of society. There was even an eight-page, full-color photo spread in *Life* magazine that featured the work of Lloyd Kahn and Steve Baer. Domes were everywhere—as restaurants, laboratories, offices, churches, and, of course, homes. Domes were no longer reserved for a few. They were feasible for everyone.

To match the growing public demand, a commercial interest in dome building was born. For those not mechanically inclined or without the time to do all the work themselves, this new industry provided precut dome kits that could be put together by the owner or built by a contractor. In these kits 2

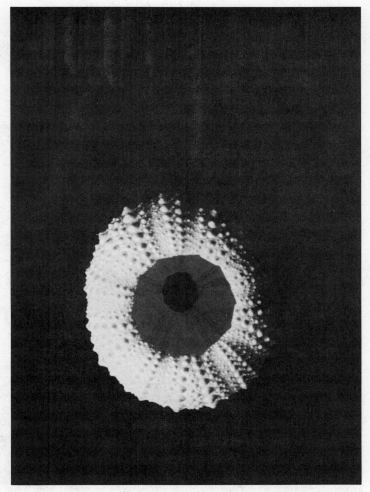

X 4's were usually cut to the required lengths and angles for the struts, then glued and nailed to exterior half-inch plywood to form the necessary pentagons and hexagons.

Pease Woodwork developed the earliest dome kits and licensed the business to other manufacturers. Three of these—Cadco, Price and Rutzebeck, and Geodesic Manufacturing—formed the Geodesic Dome Manufacturers' Association and set up dealerships and displays throughout the country.

Meanwhile, in Phoenix, Bill Woods' Dyna Domes produced fiberglassed plywood dome home kits, and in Albuquerque, Steve Baer's Zomeworks, founded in 1969 to build solar heating units, designed structures derived from polyhedra Baer calls zonahedra. These pioneering organizations were the beginnings of a minor industry, one that is still very young but growing very rapidly.

THE ROLE OF THE DOME

As a shape, the dome goes back to the beginnings of man and society; it may also play an important role in our future architectural forms. But no matter which period of time we consider, the dome is usually associated with shelter, security, stability, and an overall sense of well-being.

The dome has always had a symbolic, religious, and cosmic meaning, and just looking around any city it's easy to see the way this tradition has continued. Churches immediately come to mind—and mortuaries. But then look again; dome shapes seem to appear more and more frequently as we look for them. Hospitals often have domes, as do libraries, schools, and government buildings.

Permanence is another of the dome's unshakeable themes. In the past, this has been achieved in large, traditional buildings whose shapes symbolized certain things for people all over the world. Today the dome has a more active role; its place in contemporary housing has brought it back to the personal level where it began.

In terms of design, the dome is the strongest and most durable of architectural forms—a dome was the only structure to withstand the direct blast of the atomic bomb at Hiroshima. Perhaps if Buckminster Fuller's instincts are wrong, such a dome will be all that remains of our civilization. On the other hand, domed-over cities and giant geodesic spheres might also come to symbolize the brighter side of our future.

Fuller's Expo dome after fire.

Chapter 2. Are You a Potential Dome Home Owner?

The dome is a highly specialized form of housing. As with any design that's so refined, a number of its benefits come only at the expense of the benefits you might find in other designs. An interest in saving money on gasoline rules out an interest in an oversized car, and an interest in a dome home rules out an interest in a lot of walls and small rooms. It's pretty easy to tell whether a dome appeals to you personally, but there are a number of things you ought to think about in deciding whether or not a dome fulfills your housing needs. This chapter, and the next two, will give you an idea of what's involved.

SOME THINGS TO REMEMBER ABOUT DOMES

Because of the dome's symmetrical geometric form, its shape can't be altered to a great extent. You can distort a dome elliptically in a horizontal or a vertical direction, creating either an oblate spheroid or what looks like part of an egg standing on end. You can also raise a dome or sink some of it below ground level. These are just about the only ways a dome can be integrated into a building site. Though few other forms blend with certain natural settings as well as the dome, your site should be chosen very carefully because of these limitations.

The design of the dome accounts for its great load-bearing capacity as well as its structural stability. But this positive quality can be lost if you have to add to your original dome. Unlike additions to standard dwellings, which can be attached fairly easily, additions that cut into the structural members of a dome can weaken the framework.

Remember too that the dome's entire outer surface is exposed. This necessitates highly professional roofing and sealing techniques, especially since daily temperature changes subject domes to a lot of expansion and contraction. In addition, the surface of the dome is heated unevenly as the sun strikes the surface in different areas throughout the day. If this isn't taken into account, expansion and contraction can produce serious leakage problems, as well as a bit of creaking. Domes are often criticized because it's difficult to fit appliances and other household items into the circular plan. Kit manufacturers have come up with riser walls and other innovations that have alleviated this problem somewhat, but some planning is still in order. One reason *not* to put up too many interior divisions is the great air circulation you can get in a dome. Its design is conducive to natural air flow patterns, so domes are relatively simple to heat and cool. For the same reason, noises and odors circulate easily, and this should be taken into consideration when you plan interior design, traffic patterns, and ventilation.

OTHER USES FOR DOMES

Building a home is a large-scale project, full of so many major and minor considerations that the project may sometimes prove unmanageable for the nonprofessional. And working on a dome home will only add to the challenge. However, many of these factors are minimized and some are eliminated completely when the dome is used for other purposes.

The dome is the best structure to use when large areas must be enclosed without interior divisions or interior supporting members. This is often desirable—and sometimes a necessity—for churches, museums, restaurants, theaters, sports centers, and gymnasiums. The speed with which a dome shell can be constructed is another asset in commercial building, a selling point that's highly overdramatized in residential dome building. Variations of dome forms and geodesic structures also make good covers for bulky machinery, especially when the machinery is very high or wide or must be protected under extraordinary circumstances in which the weight and balance of the enclosure is important.

Greenhouses and pool enclosures are two of the more practical uses of the dome on both a commercial and a residential level. Pool coverings—especially on a smaller scale—take advantage of solar energy to heat the water and extend the swimming season. Evaporation is also cut down, saving on water treatment chemicals as well as the water itself. And dirt, debris, and insects are less apt to get into the water and pool area. Dome greenhouses are practical for many of the same reasons. Climate can be controlled fairly easily, lengthening the growing season and enabling a greater yield of produce.

In both of these lightweight structures, perfect sealing of the seams is not an absolute necessity. There's no serious damage if the domes happen to leak a little bit. And the same structures can be used in cold weather for sunbathing. Though the temperature outside may be freezing, inside a good quality sun dome it may be over 100° F.

Domes can also be used as additions or specialty rooms for a conventional house. Since these domes are not the primary dwelling, building codes tend to be less restrictive and problems with plumbing, interior division, furnishing, and electricity may be held to a minimum. Dome porches, art studios, or offices can create a stimulating working atmosphere.

Warehouses and barns also make excellent use of the dome's spatial quality, and as the enclosures grow in size the saving in materials grows proportionately.

BUILDING CODES AND PERMITS

In building any kind of a dwelling, dome or otherwise, you'll usually have to comply with building codes and zoning regulations. Of course you can risk flamboyant noncompliance, but this involves the possibility of having your dome demolished, and it would be pretty foolish to spend so much time and effort on a project that may be destroyed as an act of "public safety." Building codes can be amazingly complicated—I've just read in the April 1977 edition of *Sunset* that more than 133 statutes apply to anyone building a house in the state of Washington. The laws in other states can be just as complicated.

As a general rule, though, the further into the country you build, the less you'll be troubled by regulations, although almost all areas of the United States are covered by some sort of building code. These regulations were originally instituted to protect the individual against poor materials and craftsmanship, but while accomplishing that, freedom of choice and even efficiency have sometimes been sacrificed.

Where a building permit is required, you'll have to contact the local building department, which will issue your building permit and go over your plans. This process may take from two to six weeks. You may have to get special permits—such as a demolition permit—and inspections, and the building department will tell you if these are necessary. If the grading of your property is to be extensive, a special grading permit may be needed, and the building permit may not be issued until the rough grading is approved.

Information required for a building permit varies from state to county to municipality. The officials within your jurisdiction will supply the necessary forms, but a few things should be kept in mind:

1. Two sets of plans and specifications are usually furnished to the building department along with the owner's and architect's name and address. The architect signs every page of both sets of plans and specifications.

2. A legal description of the property is usually required. This includes elevations, the height of floors in relation to the top of the curb (an insurance against flooded basements), the square footage of the building and the land, plus labeled boundaries showing the names of adjoining roads.

3. You must provide a plot plan that shows the location of other structures on your property.

4. A soil analysis must be done by a licensed soil engineer.

All of these plans and descriptions should be drawn to scale by a registered architect. You must submit specifications and standards on all building materials, and they must comply with local ordinances. Fire hazards are important considerations in these restrictions.

The unique engineering involved in building a dome often causes problems in obtaining permits; county and city codes can effectively discourage dome building. Many government engineers have never been exposed to space frame analysis, and they need outside help in analyzing dome plans.

You can ease this process by hiring a competent structural engineer who is licensed by the state to perform an analysis of your plans in order to assure your compliance with local codes.

My research on the acceptance of dome home construction on an official level produced some interesting, if not frustrating, results. Though there's no legislation specifically prohibiting the dome, codes, ordinances, and administrative attitudes often effectively block their construction. This means there's an even greater need for clarity, organization, and authoritative documentation when you approach this stage of the dome-building project.

In the course of assembling this book, letters of inquiry were mailed to building officials across the country. Many of these letters went unanswered. On the other hand, the Building Officials and Code Administrators International, an organization that develops codes for adoption by state and local governments, was very helpful. Since any jurisdiction can make additions, deletions, and amendments in building codes, the B.O.C.A. is trying to bring some order to the process by incorporating standard design criteria into their basic documents. B.O.C.A. publications include the *Basic Building Code,* the *Basic Mechanical Code,* the *Basic Plumbing Code,* the *Basic Fire Prevention Code,* the *Basic Housing Maintenance Code,* the *Basic Industrialized Dwelling Code,* and the *B.O.C.A. International Membership Directory.*

The B.O.C.A. has a research service that will evaluate a product or system to determine whether it's in compliance with the requirements of the *Basic Building Code.* Once found in compliance with the code, the product or system's acceptance is recommended to building officials in jurisdictions that use the B.O.C.A. code. In some cases, when a product or system has gained approval through the B.O.C.A. research and evaluation service, it's possible to circumvent the normal permit procedure when the B.O.C.A recommendation has been accepted by the appropriate building official.

ARCHITECTURAL BOARDS AND COMMITTEES

Architectural committees and review boards are rather recent innovations that may occasionally pop up in somewhat exclusive communities. Architectural boards usually consist of architects and designers who live within the particular area where a new building is being proposed. The board must be satisfied that the proposed structure will blend in with those around it, and while style is taken into consideration, the board also evaluates the soundness of the plans. Sometimes there is a fee for the services of an architectural board, but this is not all that outrageous because the board can suggest design modifications that may prove to your benefit.

You local planning department can tell you if there is such a committee in your area. If so, your plans should be submitted to them at the same time they are submitted to the building department since the committee's approval may be needed before a building permit can be issued. If you must meet with an architectural board, remember that these people have a lot of experience and expertise in their field. It's best for you to be open-minded. More important for you personally, keep in mind that the board is made up of your potential neighbors.

ORGANIZING TO CHANGE RURAL AND SUBURBAN BUILDING AND ZONING REGULATIONS

The difficulties you'll face in building your dome may be nothing compared to those you may encounter from local building officials. Because codes vary from region to region, state to state, and sometimes county to county, in policy as well as enforcement, it's impossible to say specifically how to deal with the law. However, it *is* possible for a group of owner-builders and concerned citizens to organize and effectively alter local ordinances to allow for the construction of sound alternative housing.

One such organization was established by a group of mountain dwellers in Mendocino County, California, whose homes had been declared unfit for human habitation and were tagged for demolition. Their group, which came to be known as United Stand, successfully forestalled prosecution of the people involved and promoted the acceptance of alternative lifestyles within the area. The general method of citizen participation they followed is applicable in any rural, and possibly some suburban, areas.

First, a public meeting is called. In order for the group to be effective, its specific plans and their implementation must be well defined and organized. Contact should be made with other civic groups that might have a common interest. Lines of communication must also be opened with local officials.

All this brings to government attention the fact that there's a unified body of citizens intent on exploring, understanding, and upgrading the level of building regulations in their area. Through discussion, the officials' positions can be clarified, and potential compromises can be outlined. With this information, it's possible to begin making proposals. A County Board of Supervisors should then be willing to grant a hearing.

It's important at this point to be able to identify with the local jurisdiction as a whole, as an integral part of the community. Give ample consideration to the concerns of the opposition and integrate your own proposals in a way that's as compatible as possible.

Functioning on a county level, a citizens' organization will probably produce more effective results by stressing that codes be adopted by localities rather than pushing for a change in state law. Some officials' hands are tied by a state's building code, but the more autonomous local authorities become, the more power they'll have over the local situation.

BUILDING YOURSELF OR CONTRACTING

Determining whether or not you have the skills necessary to build a house is a matter that should be resolved early and honestly. Even if it's impossible for you to complete the entire project by yourself, there are still plenty of areas where you can participate. When in doubt, it's probably best to enlist professional assistance—any financial saving or personal satisfaction gained from doing it yourself can easily be lost when you have to make costly repairs.

In order to come to a realistic decision, you should think about the demands of the task ahead. That means knowing exactly what your plans involve and having them drawn out, at least to some degree. Remember that there's a difference between being able to frame an interior and framing *the* interior, between imagining yourself doing the work and actually *doing* the work. Many times as a job progresses you'll have to make unexpected changes, and it's a little risky to have these become your on-the-job training.

Building a dome home from scratch demands a tremendous amount of skill, and all but the most accomplished builders are often advised against it. This doesn't mean there aren't any difficulties involved in building with manufactured kits; they're also a major undertaking.

Consider the scale of the project for just a few moments, think about how it unfolds step by step, how the completion of one phase can lead to the start of two others, and so on. The fact that the housing industry itself is so large clearly illustrates the point that for one reason or another most people cannot build their own homes.

But don't be completely discouraged. Desire is an important factor, as it is in any major undertaking. A half-hearted attempt resulting in half a house is more a liability than it is a home. If you're motivated to educate yourself and learn about the home-building process, you can learn to solve problems where there is no easy solution and get help when you know you need it.

Objective self-evaluation is important. There may be tasks involved that you haven't tackled before but can manage fairly easily. Then again, there are others you may initially feel capable of performing that become something else when you actually have to do them. Your own past performance is probably the best point of reference for an evaluation of your skills. Being able to fix leaky pipes and change worn washers doesn't necessarily certify you to run a plumbing system.

There's really no set formula for determing to what degree a person can participate in an owner-built home—so many variables come into play. However, the construction of a dome house requires a greater degree of talent and expertise than most conventional structures do. The shape itself is very demanding.

Having some cabinetwork in your background is a definite advantage. Cabinetmakers are accustomed to thinking in terms of allowances for expansion and contraction and must have an eye for potential warpage. They're also familiar with the precision in cutting materials and joining that comes into play in dome building. Any knowledge or firsthand experience with building boats is also a plus factor. The experience with curvilinear shapes gained in building seaworthy craft can come in very handy on any dome project.

Of course, a high level of carpentry expertise is very valuable, especially considering the many angle cuts that may be necessary for struts, interior and exterior sheeting, and flooring. After a few hours of measuring and cutting, angles and lengths can become very confusing, and you'd be surprised how easy it is to cut the wrong angle on the wrong end of a piece of wood.

You can see, then, that establishing whether or not you're capable of handling a dome project, be it from scratch or with the help of kits, is certainly not easy. Ken Kern, a well-known and widely respected builder and designer from Oakhurst, California, has devised a test to help you sort out the answers. Mr. Kern is the author of *The Owner Built Home* and *The Owner Built Homestead,* and is also a mason, surveyor, and architect. For many years he's been deeply involved researching and developing alternative methods of dwelling construction, and some of his contributions have appeared in *Mother Earth News, Green Revolution, Organic Gardening,* and *Shelter.* His test will tell you whether or not you would enjoy do-it-yourself homebuilding and how successful your efforts might be. It gives an idea of your abilities in the various construction phases and shows what kind of jobs you can successfully handle yourself and what jobs you should hire out.

Take the test, answering each question as objectively as you can. Score your answers after each of the four sections. Then determine your final test results to see if you have what it takes to build your own home.

KEN KERN'S HOME BUILDERS' TEST

Part One. Personal

Do-it-yourself homebuilding is a very personal way of getting your own home, since it depends upon your knowledge, your skill, your energy, your wants, your finances and your determination. You'll need certain personal attributes for success. Actually they're not so different from the requirements for success in many other undertakings.

1. Are you in good physical condition? Are you free of physical impairments, such as a bad back, that would make it difficult or risky for you to work from a ladder or scaffolding or to lift fairly heavy objects? (*Yes* counts 10 points.)

2. Are you strong enough to carry a 94-pound sack of cement or a heavy plank for short distances? (*Yes* counts 1 point.)

3. Do you tire easily when working on your feet? (*No* counts 1 point.)

4. Are you young and vigorous or, if not, would you be able to hire help with the heavy physical work, such as digging? (*Yes* counts 1 point.)

5. Are you "accident prone?" (*No* counts 3 points.)

6. Do you have much free time in which to work on a home project? Evenings? Weekends? (10 points if you have at least 20 hours a week free.)

7. Do you want a home of your own enough to give up most of your leisure time for a year or more to build it? (*Yes* counts 10 points.)

8. Would you also be willing to give up many of your social activities for a while in order to provide additional time to build your own home? (Give yourself 5 points for a *yes*.)

9. Do you have the will power to make yourself work, even when you might rather be doing something else? (5 points if you answered *yes*.)

10. Would you be able to count on help from your family or friends, even if only someone to hold the other end of a board, or to help drive nails? (3 points for a *yes*.)

11. Do you LIKE to make things yourself? (Put down 10 points if you answered *yes*.)

12. Have you ever wished for something worthwhile to do during your spare time—something that would get you and your family ahead? (A *yes* here is worth 1 point.)

13. Would you take pride in building your own home and showing it to friends, or would you be just as happy with one that a contractor had built? (1 point for a *yes* to the first question.)

14. Do you have a record of successful planning and carrying out of projects on your job or at home? These could be in any field, the important thing is that you carried them through to successful completion. (*Yes* is 5 points.)

15. Do you find it easy to keep busy in your spare time without a boss over you? (3 points for this one if you answered *yes*.)

16. Would you or your family mind living in an unfinished house for a time if it were necessary to save on rent money? (*No* is 3 points.)

17. Do you have a vacant lot to build on, or the money to buy one? If not, would you be willing to sell your car, or something else of sufficient value, to buy a lot free and clear? (10 points for a *yes* to this important question.)

18. Do you have a good credit standing so that you could qualify for a loan, or would you be willing to build a little at a time as you have cash for materials? (10 points for a *yes* here.)

19. Is your income sufficient that you could meet the payments on a mortgage? (10 points if you answered *yes* to this.)

20. If you are now paying rent, could you afford both the rent and your mortgage payment for a time until your new home was livable and you could move into it? You often are allowed up to three months without payments on a do-it-yourself home loan. (1 point for a *yes* to this.)

This was the most limiting part of the test and you must score high on it to be qualified for the rest. If you're not personally suited to do-it-yourself homebuilding, no amount of construction aptitude will get you through.

The *must* questions are numbers 1, 6, 7, 11, 17, 18 and 19. If you scored on ALL of them for a score of 70 or more, you ARE personally suited to building your own home. But if you missed on even one of these key questions, count do-it-yourself homebuilding as a doubtful risk for you, at least until you can change things.

Add up your score on this section before you go on to the next. Score 70—passing, 80—good, 90—excellent, 100—superior.

Part Two. Visualization

The ability to think in terms of three-dimensional properties is called structural visualization. Everyone is believed to possess either structural or its opposite abstract visualization—one or the other, but not both.

Both have their advantages, but structural visualization is needed for do-it-yourself homebuilding. Most people are "structural" thinkers and it's doubtful whether anyone without structural visualization would be happy building a "structural" project as large as a house. See if any of these ring a bell for you:

21. Are you a fan of put-together-take-apart puzzles? (1 point if you are.)

22. Are you good at working mazes? Jigsaw puzzles? (½ point each, if you're good.)

23. Do you often try to figure out how certain things are put together and perhaps want to take them apart to find out? (1 point for a *yes*.)

24. Can you walk through someone's home and later sketch out a rough floor plan of the room arrangement? (5 points if you can.)

25. Can you draw a sketch of something you want to build and follow the sketch as you build it? (A *yes* gives you 5 points on this one.)

26. Can you read blueprints? (*Yes* is 5 points.)

27. Would you rather do research for a treatise on the workings of color television or on the effectiveness of television commercials? (2 points for *workings*.)

28. Does your work deal with the concrete or the abstract? If both, at which part do you excel? (5 points for the concrete.)

29. Do you like working with wood? (A *yes* answer counts for 3 points.)

Since you either HAVE structural visualization or you don't have it, you may claim all 20 points on this portion of the test if you scored 7 or better, or if you are certain by other indications that you possess structural visualization.

Part Three. Carpentry

There is something basic about the nature of homebuilding, and carpentry—the building of the actual structure out of wood—is probably the most basic and often the most enjoyable part of homebuilding. A house takes shape quickly, giving a stimulating feeling of great accomplishment. Needed is the ability to work with the hands and to measure, cut, and fit together the pieces that make up the structure. The techniques can be learned by reading and by asking questions. If you would like a home of your own enough to learn, don't worry if you cannot claim credit on every question.

30. Are you good with a hammer and nails? (1 point if you are.)

31. Can you saw a board along a line? (Give yourself 1 point if you can.)

32. Can you read a rule or tape measure? (Score 1 point for a *yes* to this. Actually, this is a skill that can be developed through practice.)

33. Can you read blueprints? (Here's THAT one again. Only 3 points this time.)

34. Give yourself half a point for each of these carpentry tools you own: hammer, saw, square, two-foot or longer level, plumb line, chalk line, set of chisels, 6-foot or longer steel tape measure or 6-foot folding rule, linoleum knife, hand plane, hand drill, brace and bits (or wood bits for electric drill), putty knife, carpenter's framing square.

35. Take one point for each of these power tools you have: electric drill, portable saw, sander, drill press, bench or table saw, bandsaw, jigsaw, radial saw, shaper, jointer-planer, router, wood lathe, grinder. (You could build a home without using any of these tools; they make the job quicker and easier—and they indicate your interest in building things.)

36. Chalk up half a point for each of these simple projects you have built that turned out well: plastic scale model, doghouse, sandbox, other simple projects.

37. Score one point for each of these you have built that turned out successfully: boat, cabinet or other piece of furniture, wall or partition, steps, wooden fence, wooden scale model, other involved project of wood.

38. Have you ever built a garage or room addition? (Give yourself ten points if you were in charge and if it turned out well. Three points if you helped with the carpentry.)

39. Would you tear out a wall you spent several hours building if you discovered that it was not

straight? (Score 3 points if quality won out.)

40. Do you know someone you can go to for advice on carpentry when you need it? (Take 3 points if he is a good source of accurate information.)

41. Are you willing to read, listen and learn about the principles of carpentry? (3 points if you are.)

Add up your score for this section. Score 13—passing, 20—good, 27—excellent, 35—superior.

The important thing to remember is that if your score is low, you should have answered yes to question 41 because you have some extra work ahead of you learning about carpentry. If you scored "excellent" or "superior," you should have few problems with carpentry, which represents a large part of the labor on your home.

If you score less than 13 on this section, you'd do well to hire a skilled carpenter, at least to advise you and to inspect your work on a do-it-yourself home project.

Part Four. Mechanical

While similar to carpentry, the mechanical aspects of homebuilding require further knowledge. These are the electrical wiring, plumbing, heating and concrete work. They all can be learned by reading and by asking questions, but this part of the test will indicate how much you already know. Not many people would be able to successfully answer it all, so don't worry if you miss some.

42. Have you ever tinkered with old clocks or other such mechanical contraptions? (1 point if you're a good tinkerer.)

43. Have you had any luck assembling children's toys from instructions? (A Christmas Eve mechanic earns 2 points.)

44. Who fixes things at your house when they break? (1 point if it's you.)

45. Have you ever repaired an electrical device, such as an iron, a toaster, or a lamp? (Score 1 point if you have.)

46. Do you do any of your own car repairs? (Take 3 points for a *yes* on this one.)

47. Have you ever overhauled an automobile engine? (Give yourself 5 points on this if you were in charge, 2 points if you helped someone else do it.)

48. Have you done any electrical wiring work, such as building a radio or wiring a doorbell? (Credit yourself 3 points for each such project.)

49. Ever done any electrical wiring around the house? (Give yourself 3 points for each of these jobs you did: added electrical receptacles to house system, installed ceiling or wall light outlet, wired switching circuits, added a new circuit either with armored cable or nonmetallic cable and outlet boxes, added an outdoor light by wiring it into the house electrical system, wired a room addition or garage.)

50. Have you ever built any sizable project using concrete, brick, or block? (Take 1 point if you helped a friend; 3 points if you ran the job.)

51. Score half a point for each of these "mechanical" tools you have: pliers, screwdrivers of assorted sizes, tin snips, wire-cutters, pair of pipe wrenches, soldering iron or gun, propane torch, adjustable open-end wrench, cold chisel, hacksaw, tubing cutter, mason's trowel, concrete trowel, concrete float, socket wrench set, concrete drill, pipe cutter, pipe dies. (While not all of these are needed to build a house, they are an indication of your interest in mechanical things.)

52. Are you willing to learn by asking questions and reading about electrical wiring, plumbing, heating, concrete work, and masonry? (Take 3 points for a *yes*.)

Add up your score for this section. Score 13—passing, 20—good, 27—excellent, 35—superior. Here, as in the carpentry section, if your score is low you must be willing to learn. If your score is "excellent" or "superior," you should have no trouble doing the mechanical jobs in building a home of your own. If you score less than 13 on this section, consider hiring out the mechanical jobs on your do-it-yourself home, or at least having the help of skilled craftsmen in these lines.

Final Score

Add up your individual scores on all four sections of the test and find your overall test results below. In every case you should have gotten a minimum of 70 on the Personal section and credit for all 20 points of the Visualization section, as described at the end of it.

116—Barely passing. Look over your individual scores to see where you are weak and decide whether you want (1) to build your own home enough to work at improving your ability, (2) to hire out some of the work or (3) to work under the supervision of skilled craftsmen, doing the easy, routine jobs yourself to save money.

140—A good score, especially if you maintained a passing grade or better in both the Carpentry and Mechanical sections. If you want, you can build your own home and do a job that you'll be proud to show friends.

165—You are well qualified as a do-it-yourself homebuilder and need have no hesitation about whether you can do it.

190—You have mastered yourself and the

abilities you'll need to build your own home and save. You should get a great deal of pleasure out of being a home owner-builder and it should be easy for you, particularly if you scored high on the Personal section.

MANUFACTURERS, CONTRACTORS, AND CONTRACTS

The primary role of any dome home manufacturer is to supply the consumer with a product. It's not the manufacturer's responsibility to protect the interests of the consumer—it's the consumer's responsibility to determine exactly which manufacturer's contracts and services are best suited to his or her personal needs. There's a great variety of products and services available, and the contracts that bind the consumer to these financial investments are just as varied.

You should make a thorough investigation of any manufacturer you're thinking of doing business with, and cross-reference it through as many sources as possible. A local distributor should be checked through the company's main office. If they're willing, have the company put you in touch with customers they've served. Research the materials they supply. Read books about prefabricated homes. (One that evaluates and explains many systems other than domes is the *Handbook of Housing Systems for Designers and Developers* by Laurence Stephan Cutler and Sherrie Stephens Cutler.) Examine all contracts carefully, and before committing yourself to anything, get an attorney.

Some companies simply supply the consumer with a kit, and from the point the contract is signed the builder is totally alone. Think about what this means and be sure your capabilities measure up to the task ahead. In this case, the owner must secure all permits; perform all the labor; provide the exterior and interior finishes; assemble all the building materials; be responsible for footing, foundation, and any excavation work, and much, much more. Kits like this may well be worth the price, but remember that you're buying materials and banking on your own capabilities to complete the major part of the project.

Some dome home manufacturers will not deal directly with the consumer, preferring to sell on a wholesale basis only to professionals. The manufacturer's responsibilities in these instances lie with the builder. The consumer deals directly with the builder, and the manufacturer is not under any contractual obligation to the consumer. There are good

reasons why some manufacturers choose this marketing method. Professional results can be expected from contractors with direct experience in building domes. The consumer is saved the problem of finding a contractor willing to build a dome, and the contractor doesn't need to be taught any special building techniques. A contractor who is unfamiliar with domes will take longer to complete the project, and it will cost more money. His margin for error is greater than that of a contractor familiar with dome building. However, once familiar with the plans, there is no reason why any competent contractor should have any major difficulties erecting a dome.

In between these two approaches are the manufacturers who sell to the consumer with options on various services. They may supply as little as the bare shell or as much as a fully completed dome, all depending on the desires of the consumer. They may offer design services to adapt basic plans to personal tastes and assist with decorating, laying out, and integrating interior divisions. Site planning services may also be provided. For the owner-builder who wishes to have some involvement in building but not take on the whole project, an arrangement like this would be a wise move.

The contractor can make all the arrangements for the construction of your dome—overseeing the project; maintaining the construction schedule; finding, coordinating, and dealing with the subcontractors necessary for the job. Subcontractors and other employees are usually paid from the contractor's fees.

The procedure for finding a contractor varies with the manufacturer and the way you choose to approach the construction. In the event that you deal with a manufacturer who offers no other services, finding a contractor will be up to you. The best source of information is people who have recently built in the area and, better yet, people who have contracted for dome construction. Builders' associations can also provide valuable information about contractors and answer almost any questions you might have.

When you've narrowed down the field, you should thoroughly check out any contractor you're thinking of hiring. If asked for references, he will usually only give you the names of people he feels will extol his virtues. Banks, mortgage companies, and local building departments often have more reliable information about particular builders, but they're sometimes unwilling to part with this, and they're certainly under no obligation to do so.

However, the local building department *does* have a list of people who have received building permits over the past few years. This list is public property and it shows the names of home owners and their respective contractors. From this list you can determine how busy a contractor is and find the names of people he has dealt with who may not have been included in his list of references.

When you choose a general contractor, the next step is to draw up a contract for the construction. Remember to take these points into consideration:

1. The contractor must see to it that all work shown in the building plans and described in the specifications is performed.

2. The contract should include a specific date for completion of the project.

3. A specific figure to be paid the contractor should be included in the agreement, plus the method in which payment is to be made. If payment is to be made at the completion of various stages of work, the specific stages and the amount due should be stated exactly.

4. The contractor pays for all power, tools, labor, equipment, and all facilities needed to complete the job.

5. The contractor must abide by all the laws, ordinances, and codes that apply to the building project, and he is responsible for obtaining all licenses and permits necessary to finish the construction and secure occupancy.

6. The contractor should assume liability for any loss or damage to the owner's property where the loss is the result of the contractor's negligence or that of his employees.

7. The contractor should carry workmen's compensation insurance to cover for injuries suffered by his employees in connection with completion of the project, and subcontractors should carry similar insurance.

8. The contractor should assume liability and be responsible for any injuries, including any to the owner and the owner's family, that are the result of his omissions or those of any of his subcontractors or employees. For this, the

contractor should carry public liability insurance.

9. The contractor should be willing to show the owner proof that such insurance is being carried.

10. The contractor should at all times keep the premises clean—this is especially important during periods of inspection—and when the job is completed all trash, tools, surplus material, and equipment should be removed from the property.

11. The owner should have fire insurance and extended coverage to 100 percent of the entire structure's value, and this should include all materials, both surplus and those used for the permanent structure. This coverage should extend to any fences, protection devices, and temporary buildings used during the construction.

12. A clause should be included that allows the owner at any given time to designate in writing a person to act as his or her agent in the contract. The designated person can then be fully authorized to assume the owner's role and the contractor must accept his directions as if they were given directly by the owner.

13. When all work in keeping with the contract is finished, the contractor should notify the owner that he is ready for the owner's final inspection. When the final inspection is completed by the owner, the appropriate official inspection is passed, and the occupancy permit is granted, then and only then should final payment be made.

14. Since the contractor is in charge of paying subcontractors, in some instances it is possible for these people to put a lien against the completed structure if they haven't been duly paid. The contract should contain a clause that frees the owner from any such liens provided the owner has paid the contractor all the amounts that are due him.

15. If blasting is necessary, the contractor should be held responsible for any damage to any building, person, or property. Before blasting, the contractor should show the owner proof that insurance is being carried to cover for any such disasters.

16. The contractor should guarantee that the work has been performed to the best of his ability, and guarantee the building against defects for one year from the completion date, provided these defects are not the result of the owner's omissions or tampering. He should also

guarantee the electrical, plumbing, heating, and septic systems for one year.

17. In the event that construction is delayed by fire, poor transportation, or other unforeseen circumstances which are not the contractor's fault, the owner should agree to extend the construction period for a reasonable length of time.

18. Rights and obligations specified in the building contract should not be transferable to either owner or contractor without prior written consent. However, the contractor should be permitted to subcontract work which is covered in the contract.

19. If the contractor fails to perform his work diligently, files for bankruptcy, is judged bankrupt, or designates his property for creditors, the owner should have the option of terminating the contract and taking over the work. If this should happen, the contractor should be liable to the owner for any costs that exceed the contract. The owner should also have the right to all the machinery, materials, and any other supplies on the site that are necessary to complete the project.

20. Items to be paid for and installed by the owner should be included in the contract, as well as all items to be paid for and installed by the contractor. If allowances paid the contractor for these items exceed the total cost, the contractor should refund the owner. If the costs exceed the contractor's allowance, the owner should pay the contractor the appropriate amount.

21. The terms of any building contract should be set down fully in writing and completely understood by both parties. There should be no verbal agreements of any kind in addition to the contract, and the fact that no verbal agreements exist should be set down in writing.

22. The terms of a building contract should apply to the heirs, executors, and any persons designated by both the owner and contractor.

As you can see, the major role of the general contractor is arranging, scheduling, and dealing with the various subcontractors who perform the actual labor on the building project. If you choose to act as your own general contractor, you can save some money. But you should also be aware of the disadvantages.

For one thing, you probably won't be able to get the same consideration for discounts on building materials. Professional builders buy their materials in much greater volume than someone building an individual home. However, since you're involved in a major project, you should shop around among various materials dealers. You'll probably be able to locate one who's willing to give you a good price based on the fact that you're buying a large quantity of materials for a home.

When you're acting as your own general contractor, you must check out and negotiate with all the necessary subcontractors. You'll have to go over your plans and specifications with them and get bids from a few people within each field. You'll also have to take care of permits, insurance, and working out a construction schedule. You may have to hire a surveyor unless the mason or carpenter you hire is capable of staking out for pouring the footings. You'll have to call the building department to make inspections at the appropriate times and make sure all the payments are made on schedule.

When lending institutions are involved in a building project, there are usually three different kinds of payment plans.

In the first plan, the borrower receives the entire loan in a lump sum when the construction is completely finished. This involves a letter of commitment that binds the lender to make the loan, and this letter can then be used to get an interim loan from a bank. Some insurance companies and savings and loan companies make this type of loan, and sometimes life insurance companies will provide a letter of commitment while charging a low rate of interest on this type of loan.

Another system for disbursing funds sets up a schedule so that money is paid as the job progresses through various stages. This is called the draw system. The specific stages agreed on by the contractor and the owner; usually they include completion of the foundation, the framing inspection, and the final building inspection. Under this system, there are usually five or six stages when a draw is made against the loan and paid to the builder.

The voucher system has also become very common. This gives all parties involved a tighter control on the flow of money since individual bills are paid as they come in. This keeps the job running smoothly and the accounts payable file slender. For example, when rough plumbing has been finished, the plumber sends his invoice, and it's paid immediately. In comparison, on the draw system this bill and others may become tied up awaiting the completion of a particular building stage. The voucher system also allows the owner to put his money to use more efficiently and doesn't tie up a large amount of money.

INSPECTIONS

During the construction process, it's always a good idea to stop and take a look at the work before continuing. This is particularly important in the initial stages of dome construction, since the components are interrelated and interdependent. Depending on where you've chosen to build, it may also be a legal necessity.

Build at your own speed. This way you can be meticulous and enjoy the pride of fine craftsmanship, and also avoid any big blunders. But no matter how careful you are, you should inspect the work at certain key stages.

1. *Footings and foundations.* This inspection is critical because footings and foundations provide the support for your building. If your dome rests on wooden posts or concrete columns, they must be sunk to a depth that will bear the entire load or to bedrock, which accomplishes the same thing. The footings for continuous wall foundations will vary in dimension depending on both soil characteristics and local codes, if there are any.

Whatever kind of foundations you use, they must be sound enough to prevent the structural damage that can result from settling. Over the years, all buildings shift and settle a little, but a poorly laid foundation can ruin your entire house. In most cases where building codes apply, foundation inspections are mandatory and are carried out by an official inspector.

2. *Completion of the shell.* If you were building a traditional house, this stage is equivalent to the completion of the framing. When the skeleton of your project is completed, there's still a lot of interior and exterior work to be done, but all of this work covers the shell on both the inside and the outside, so any structural testing should be done at this point. Otherwise, if there are any problems with the shell a lot of your work may have to be torn apart to get to the source of the trouble. This can be costly as well as frustrating.

3. *Waterproofing.* Whatever your method of waterproofing, it's obviously much easier to do the job right the first time than it is to try to locate leaks when the sealing is finished. Keep in mind one rather intimidating but practical thought—the greatest waterproofing work is only as effective as the weakest point in the entire job.

4. *Plumbing.* Leaks in water pipes are most likely to pop up where the lines make sharp turns, where there happen to be a series of soldered joints, or where valves are connected. It's unusual for leaks to occur in the middle of lengths of pipe, and only very poor quality pipe could be fragile enough to be damaged during installation.

Check the plumbing system carefully because leaks will only become worse in time. When the hot water system is on, go around to each tap and check to be sure none of the lines has been accidentally reversed. As you're doing this, turn each tap on all the way, allowing as much water as possible to pass through the system. Then quickly turn off the tap. This puts a strain on the system, and if you hear a clanking thud your water pipe is vibrating and you'll have to brace it. If this isn't done, the vibration may eventually weaken a soldered joint, and a leak may result.

5. *Wiring.* You'll need two people to check the electrical system, one at a particular switch or outlet and the other to mark the switches of the circuit-breaker box. All the circuits should be carefully labeled and tested to be sure an overload hasn't been mistakenly wired through any one of them. Try loading the circuits to their maximum capacity. If the breaker switch is kicked off, you'll have to make the appropriate adjustments in your wiring.

6. *Heating.* With the great number of energy sources available, your final decision about which system or combination of systems to use should be preceded by a thorough investigation long before you actually begin construction. Obviously, your choice should be governed by the climate, plus the system's cost and its efficiency.

A Note On Architectural Drawings

Architectural drawings are the way an architect gets his thoughts down on paper. They show what he intends to do and spell out his ideas about how a particular building should be constructed. A builder can read them and estimate the costs, materials, and length of time it will take to complete the project.

But plans are just one of many steps in the building process. Their main value to a future home owner is in helping him to visualize what the finished product will be like. A layman should never try to build from plans like these without professional help—unless he wants to waste a lot of energy and money.

It takes time and practice to acquire the skills to read drawings the way professional builders and architects can, so when you look at the drawings that follow, don't drive yourself crazy trying to figure out all the details. Relax and enjoy them. You'll find that they give you a good idea of just what's involved in the

mechanics of dome construction. And if you see something you'd like to live in, get in touch with the people who drew the plans. They're in business to help take you the rest of the way.

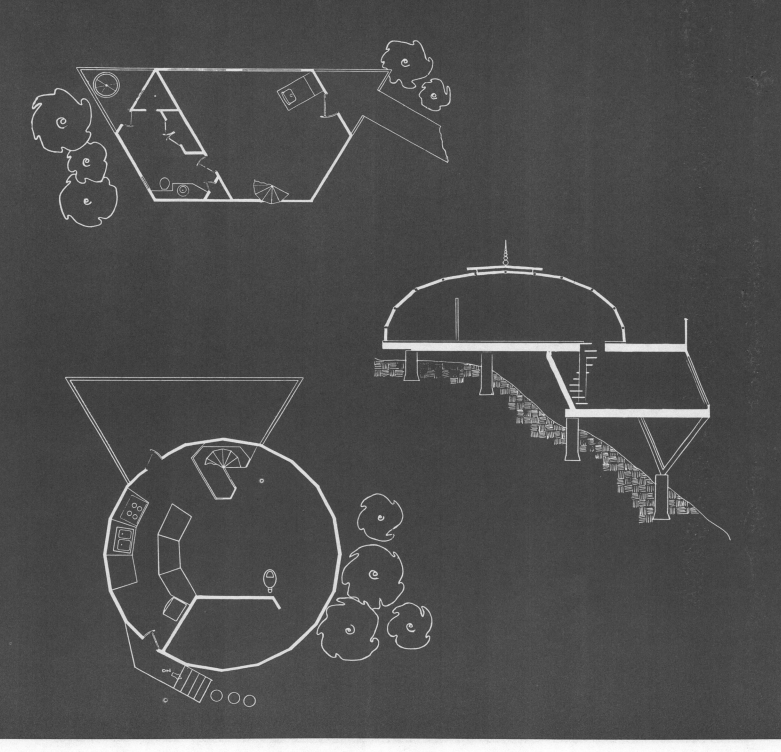

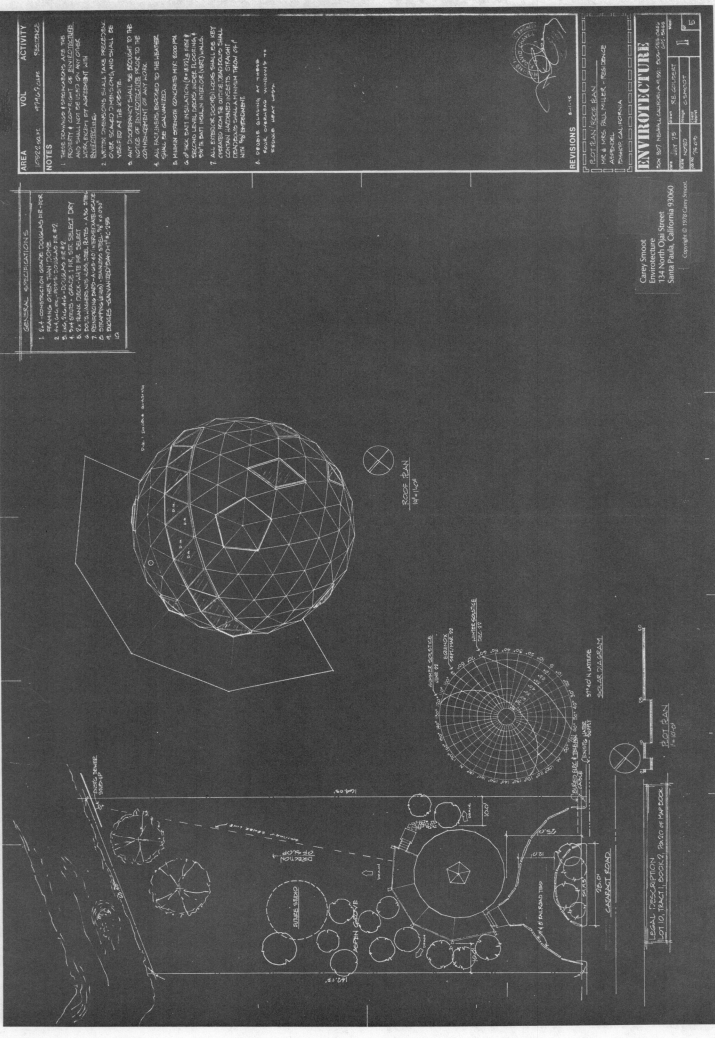

34

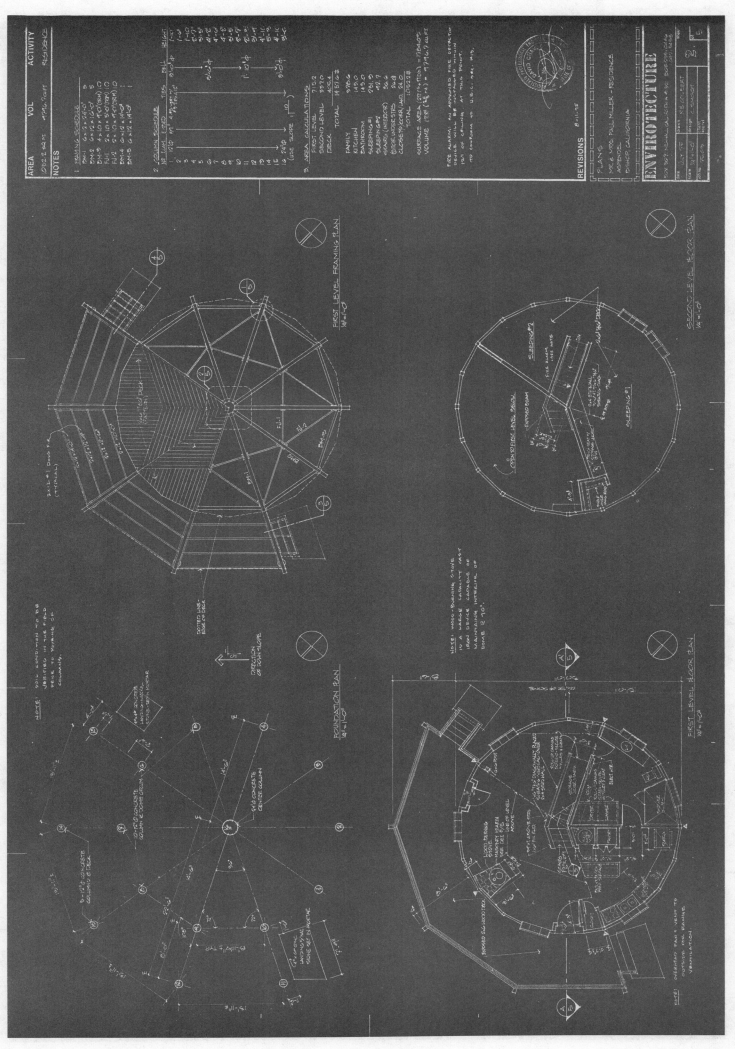

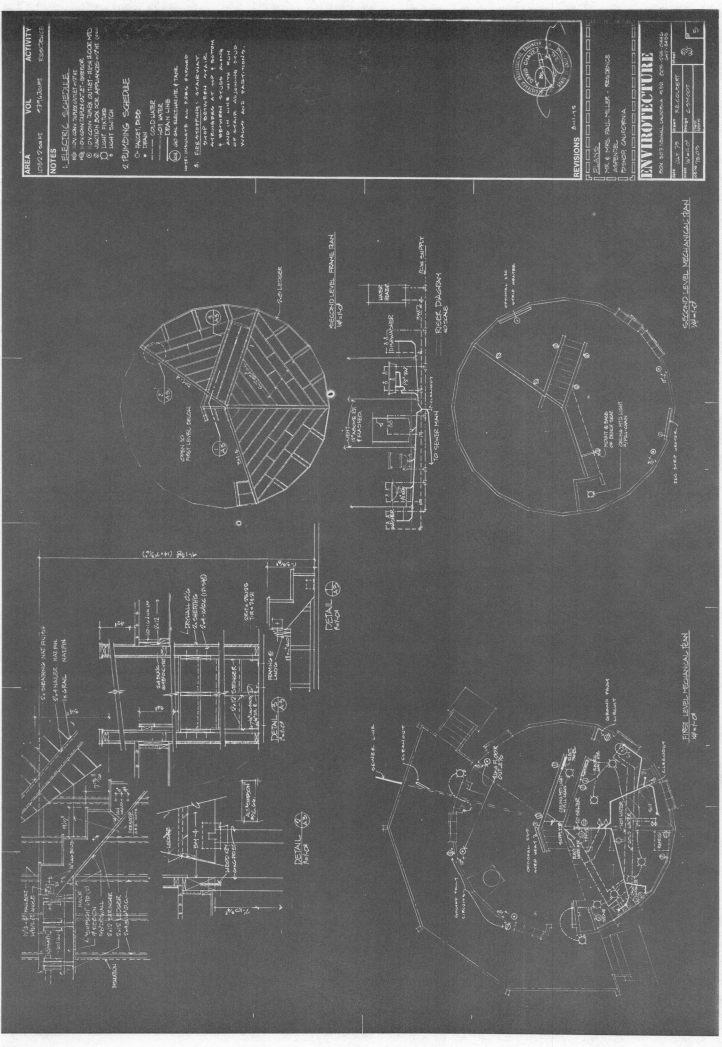

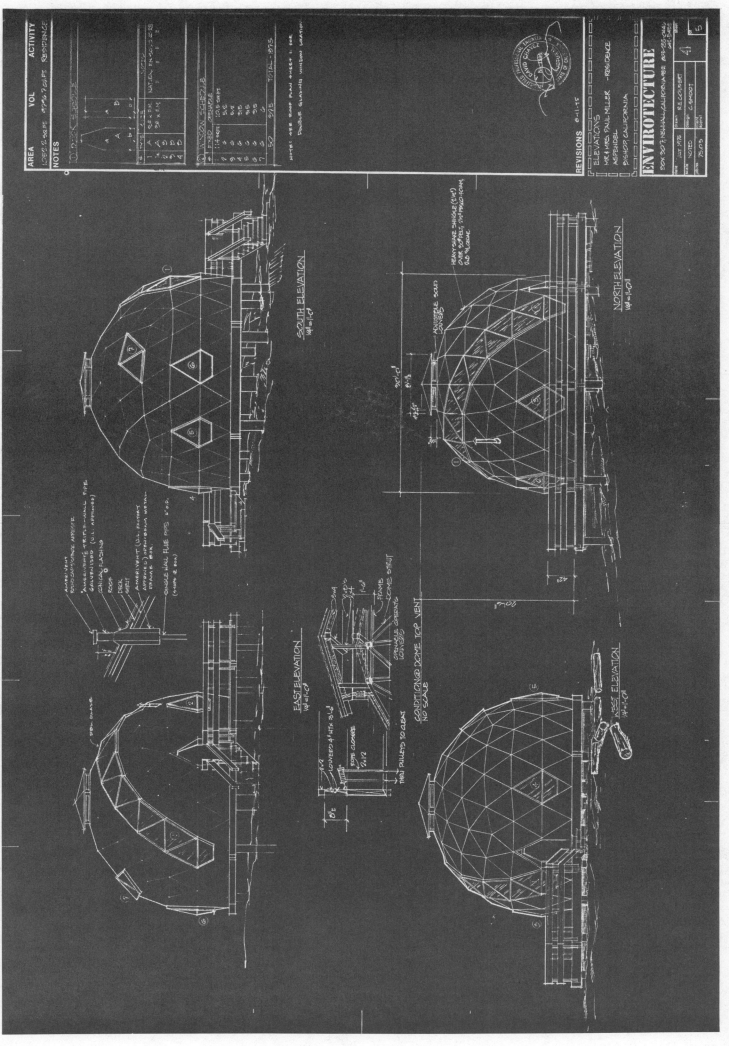

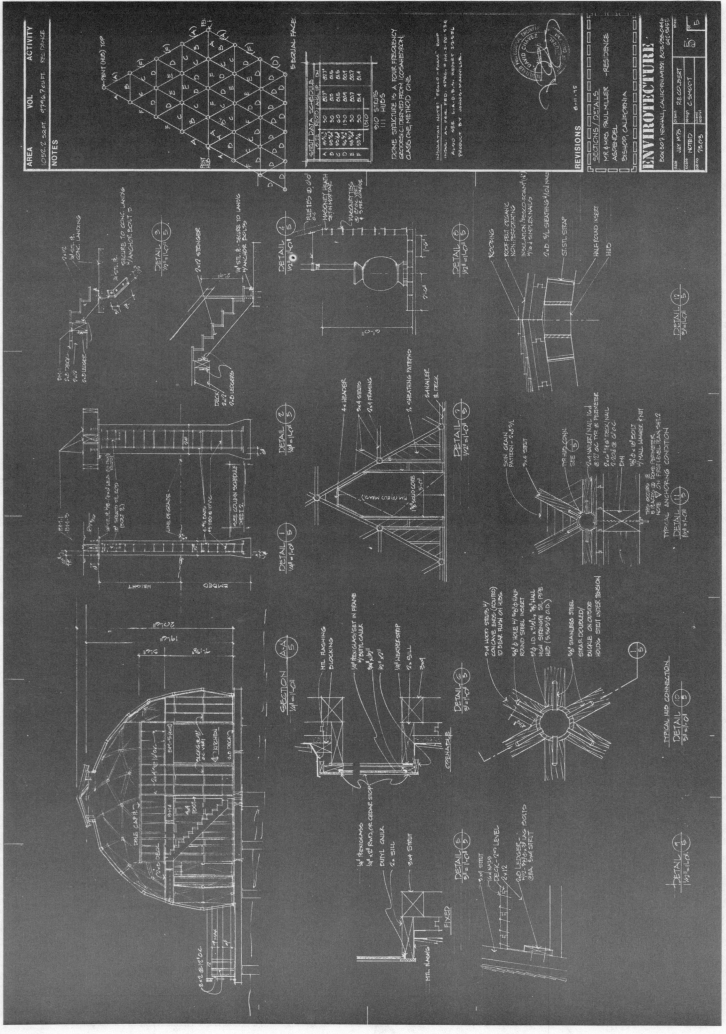

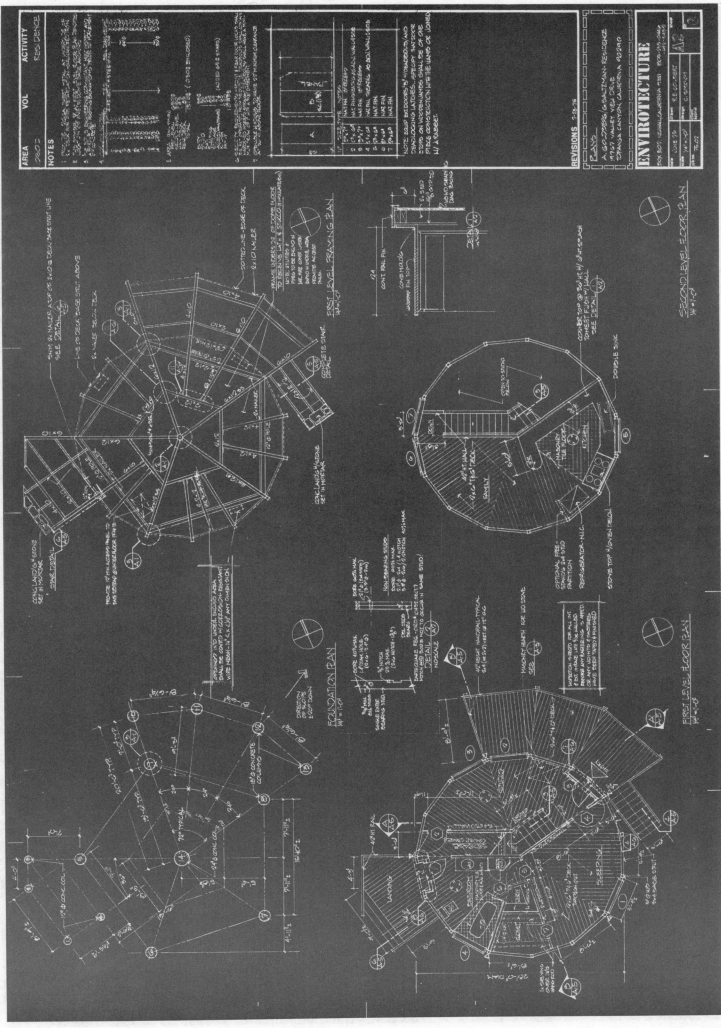

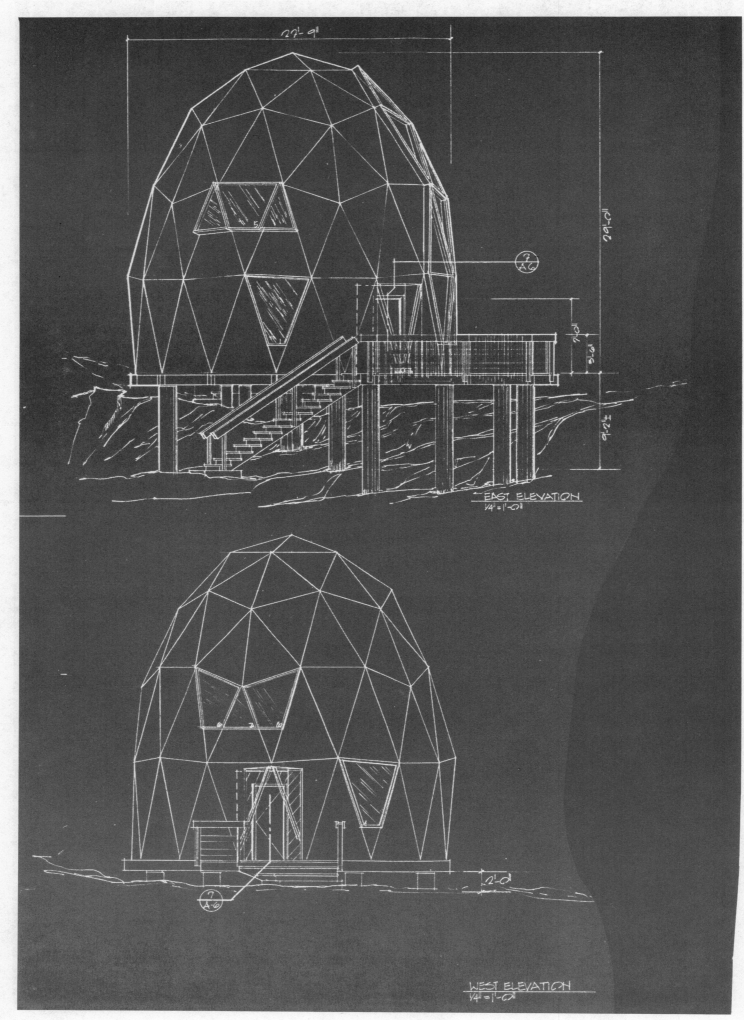

EAST ELEVATION
1/4" = 1'-0"

WEST ELEVATION
1/4" = 1'-0"

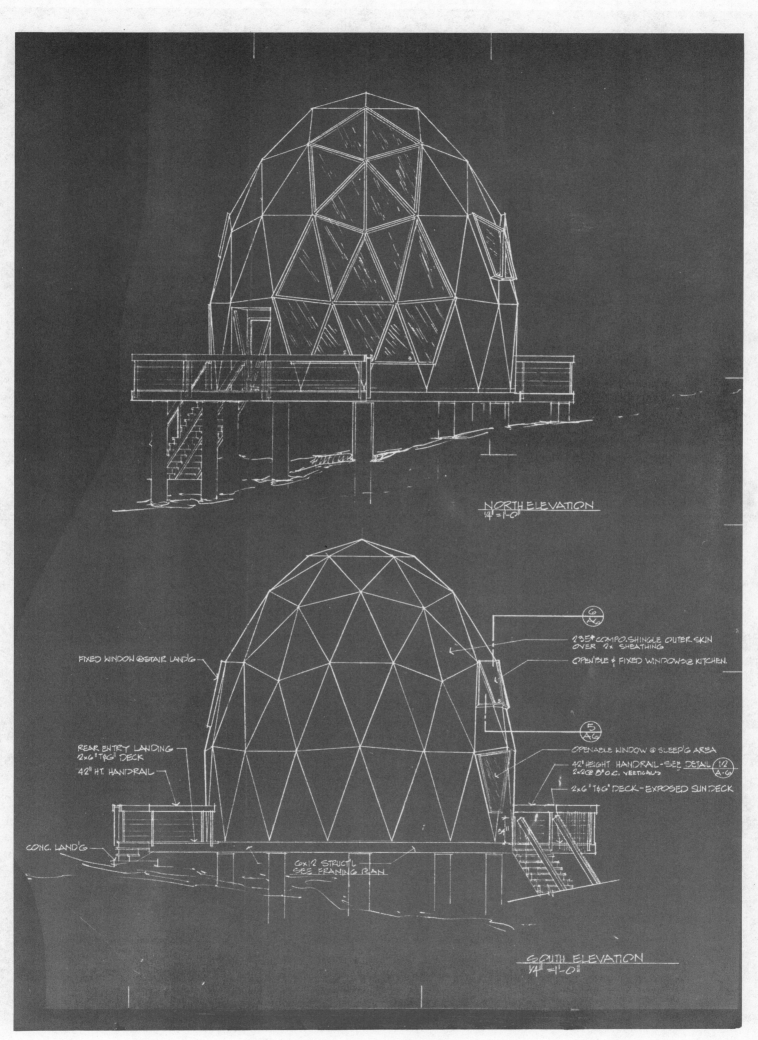

NORTH ELEVATION
1/4" = 1'-0"

235# COMPO. SHINGLE OUTER SKIN OVER 2x SHEATHING

OPEN'BLE & FIXED WINDOWS @ KITCHEN.

FIXED WINDOW @ STAIR LAND'G

OPENABLE WINDOW @ SLEEP'G AREA

42" HEIGHT HANDRAIL - SEE DETAIL 12/A-6
2x2 @ 8" O.C. VERTICALS

REAR ENTRY LANDING
2x6" T&G" DECK
42" HT. HANDRAIL

2x6 "T&G" DECK - EXPOSED SUN DECK

CONC. LAND'G

6x12 STRUCT'L
SEE FRAMING PLAN

SOUTH ELEVATION
1/4" = 1'-0"

41

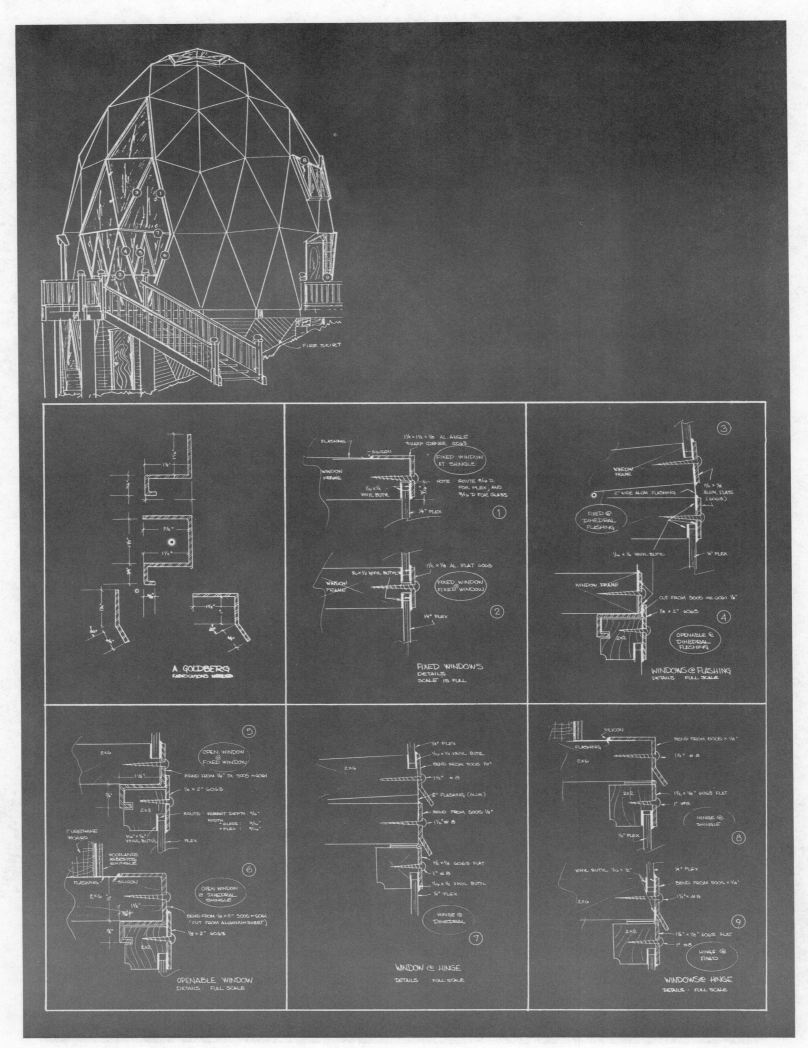

FIRE SKIRT

A. GOLDBERG
FABRICATIONS NEEDED

FIXED WINDOWS
DETAILS
SCALE IS FULL

WINDOWS @ FLASHING
DETAILS FULL SCALE

OPENABLE WINDOW
DETAILS : FULL SCALE

WINDOW @ HINGE
DETAILS FULL SCALE

WINDOWS @ HINGE
DETAILS - FULL SCALE

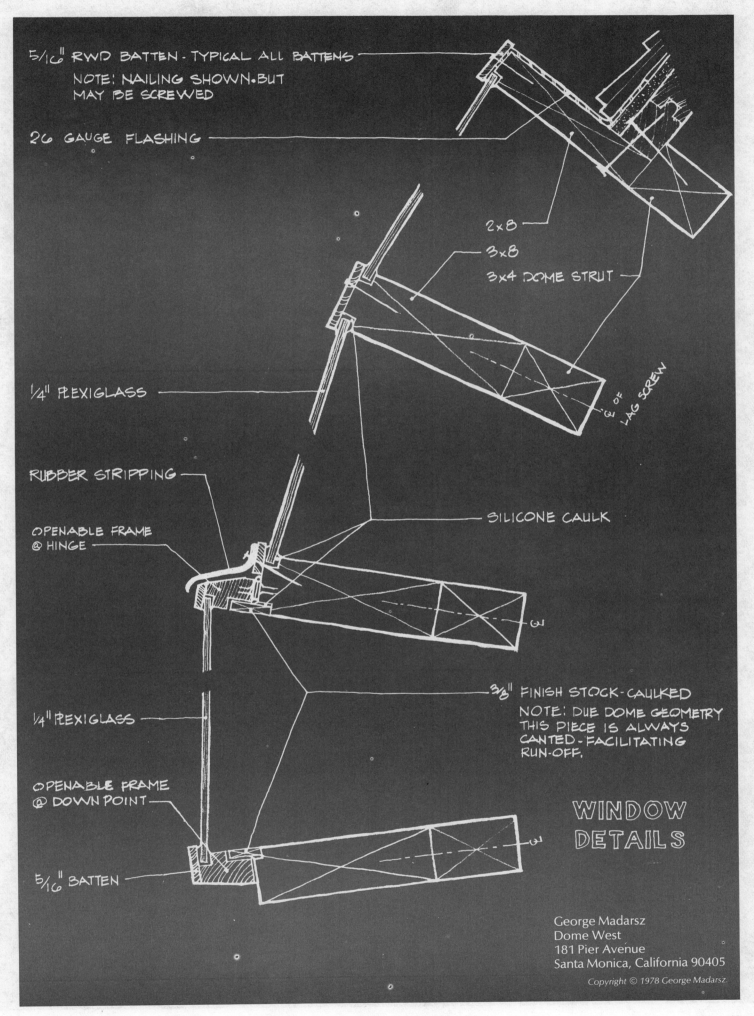

5/16" RWD BATTEN - TYPICAL ALL BATTENS

NOTE: NAILING SHOWN. BUT
MAY BE SCREWED

26 GAUGE FLASHING

2x8

3x8

3x4 DOME STRUT

¢ OF LAG SCREW

1/4" PLEXIGLASS

RUBBER STRIPPING

SILICONE CAULK

OPENABLE FRAME
@ HINGE

3

3/8" FINISH STOCK - CAULKED

NOTE: DUE DOME GEOMETRY
THIS PIECE IS ALWAYS
CANTED - FACILITATING
RUN-OFF.

1/4" PLEXIGLASS

OPENABLE FRAME
@ DOWN POINT

3

WINDOW
DETAILS

5/16" BATTEN

George Madarsz
Dome West
181 Pier Avenue
Santa Monica, California 90405

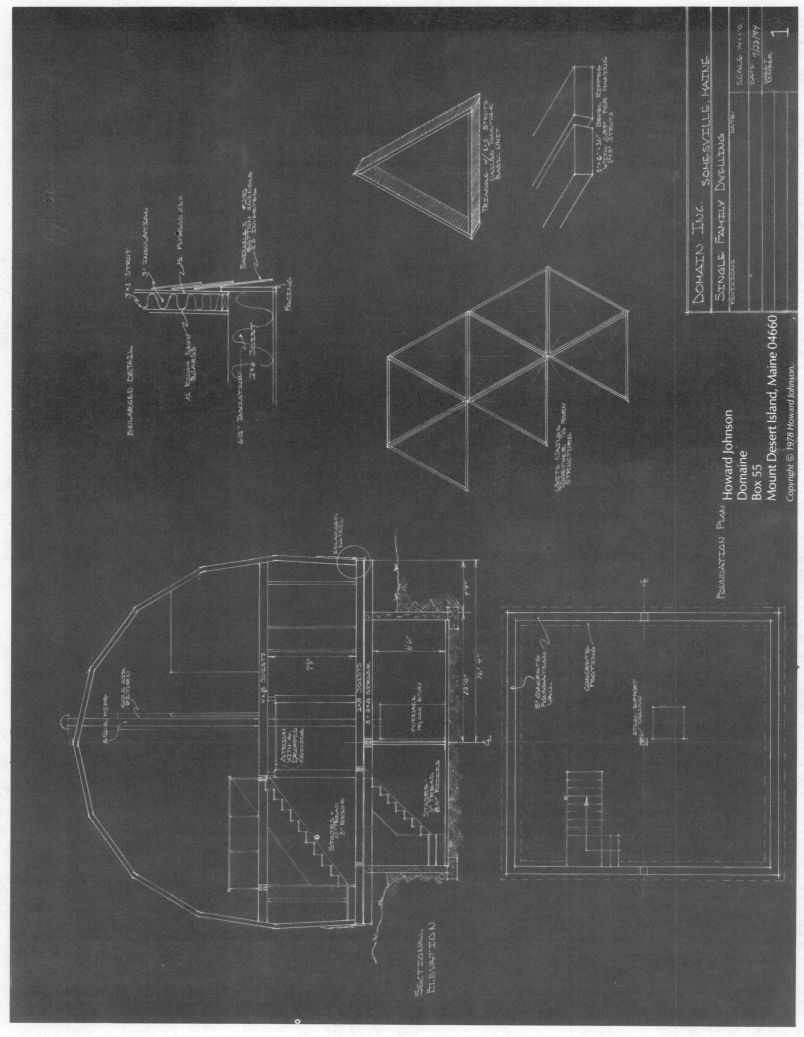

DOMAIN INC. SOMESVILLE, MAINE

SINGLE FAMILY DWELLING

REVISIONS	DATE:	SCALE 1/4"=1'0"		
		DATE 1/23/74		
		SHEET NUMBER 1		

FOUNDATION PLAN   Howard Johnson
Domaine
Box 55
Mount Desert Island, Maine 04660

ENLARGED DETAIL

SECTIONAL ELEVATION

TRIANGLE W/1½ STRUTS NAILED TOGETHER. BASIC UNIT

4"x4"x16" BEVEL RIPPED WITH LAP FOR NAILING 1½" STRUTS

UNITS NAILED TOGETHER TO FORM STRUCTURES

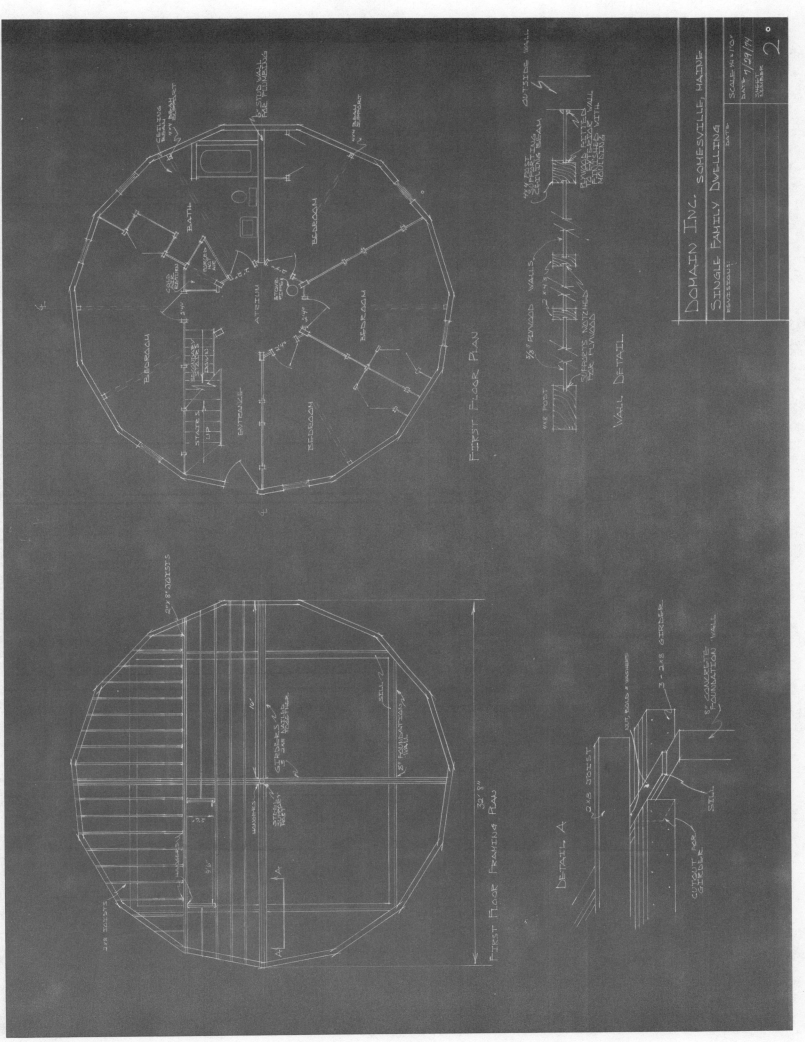

FIRST FLOOR PLAN

FIRST FLOOR FRAMING PLAN

DETAIL A

WALL DETAIL

DOMAIN INC. SOMESVILLE MAINE
SINGLE FAMILY DWELLING
SCALE 1/4"=1'0"
DATE 1/29/74
SHEET NUMBER 2

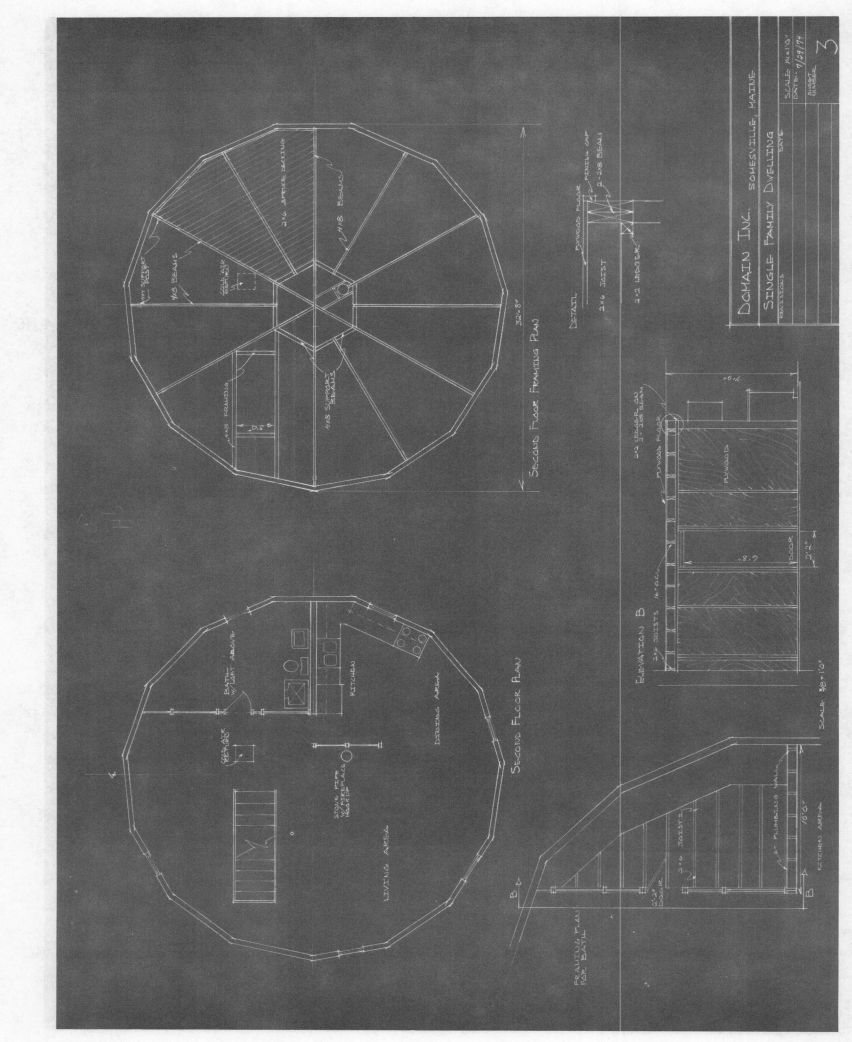

Second Floor Framing Plan

Second Floor Plan

Elevation B

SCALE ⅜"=1'0"

Detail

DOMAIN INC. SCHESVILLE, MAINE

SINGLE FAMILY DWELLING

SCALE ¼"=1'0"
DATE: 7/29/74
SHEET NUMBER: 3

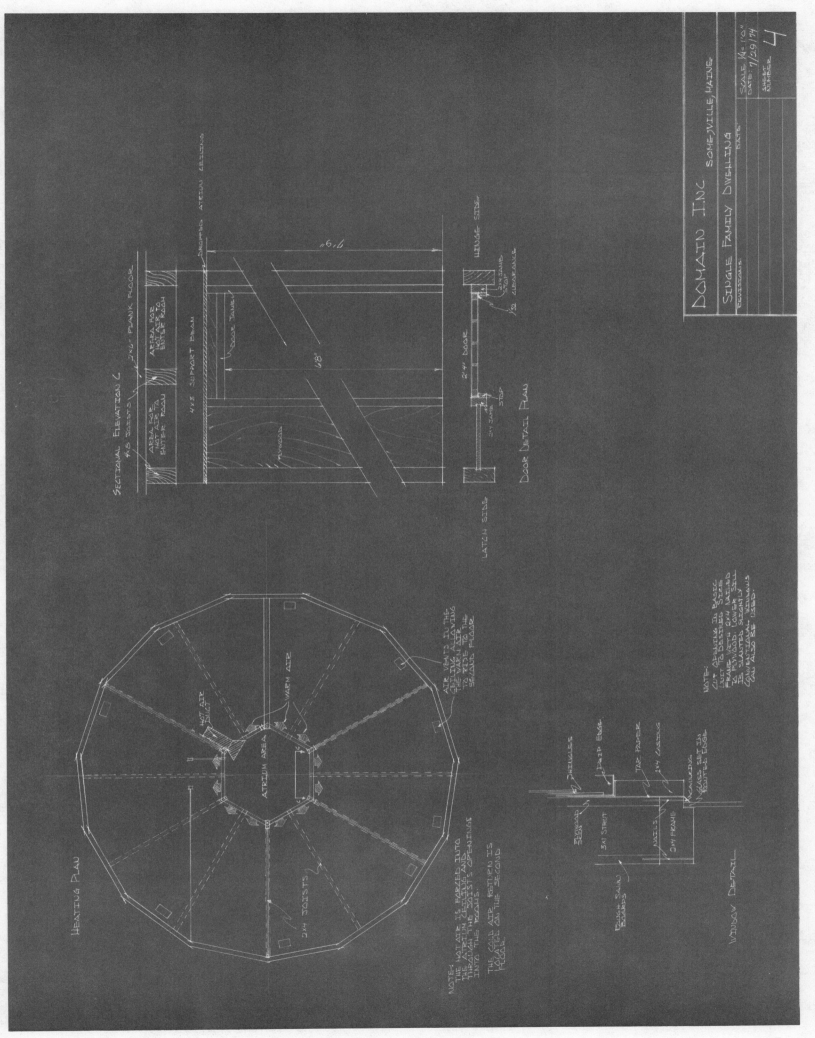

SECTIONAL ELEVATION C

4x8 JOISTS

2x6" PLANK FLOOR

AREA FOR
HOT AIR
ENTER ROOM

AREA FOR
HOT AIR
ENTER ROOM

4x8 SUPPORT BEAM

AREA FOR
HOT AIR
ENTER ROOM

DROPPED ATRIUM CEILING

6'6"

DOOR FRAME

48"

PLYWOOD

DOOR DETAIL PLAN

HINGE SIDE

2x4 JAMB

STOP

1/2 CLEARANCE

2'4" DOOR

2x4 JAMB

STOP

LATCH SIDE

HEATING PLAN

ATRIUM AREA

HOT AIR
DUCT

WARM AIR

AIR VENTS IN THE
CEILING ALLOWING
THE WARM AIR
TO THE
SECOND FLOOR

2x4 JOISTS

NOTE: HOT AIR IS FORCED INTO
THE ATRIUM CEILING AND
THROUGH THE JOISTS OPENING
INTO THE ROOMS.

THE COOL AIR RETURN IS
FLOOR LEVEL AT THE SECOND
FLOOR.

SHINGLES

DRIP EDGE

TAR PAPER

2x4 CASING

PLYWOOD

3x4 STRUT

NAILS

2x4 FRAME

GLAZING

GLASS SET IN
PUTTIED EDGE

ROUGH SAWN
BOARDS

WINDOW DETAIL

NOTE:
2x4 OPENING IN BASIC
UNIT TO DESIRED SIZES
FRAME WITH 2x4 NAILED
TO PLYWOOD LOWER SILL
IS SLANTED SLIGHTLY
CONVENTIONAL WINDOWS
CAN ALSO BE USED.

DOMAIN INC. SOMERVILLE, MAINE

SINGLE FAMILY DWELLING

ELEVATIONS

SCALE 1/4" = 1'0"
DATE: 7/29/14

SHEET
NUMBER 4

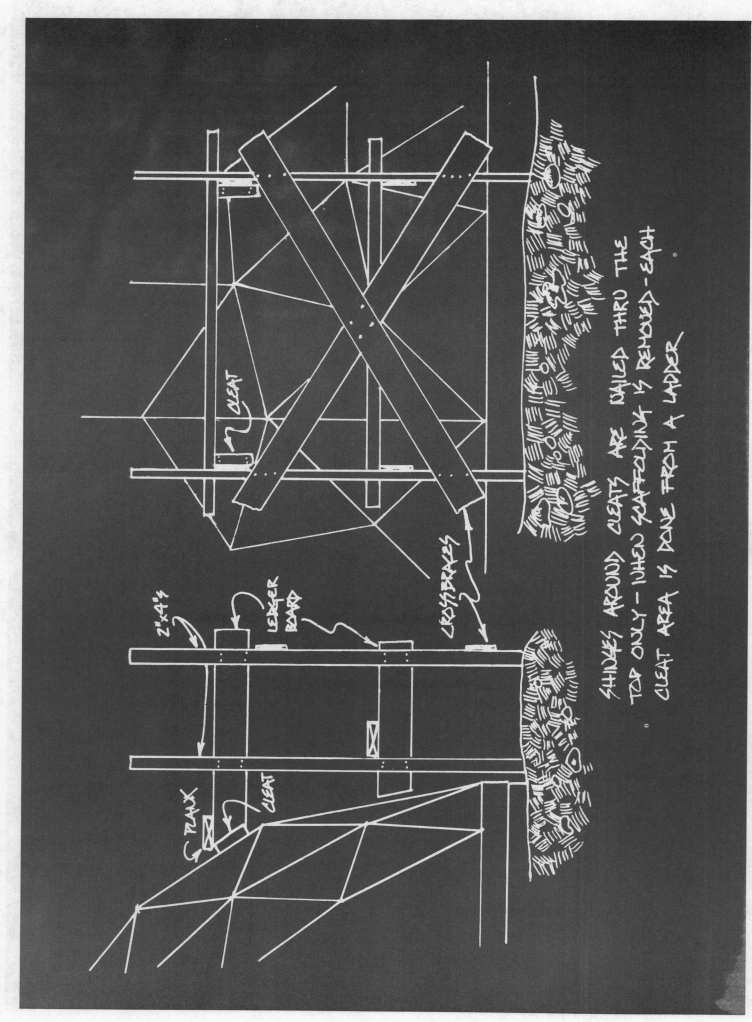

CLEAT

CLEAT

CROSSBRACES

2"x4"'s

LEDGER BOARD

PLANK

CLEAT

SHINGLES AROUND CLEATS ARE NAILED THRU THE TOP ONLY—WHEN SCAFFOLDING IS REMOVED—EACH CLEAT AREA IS DONE FROM A LADDER.

An art studio in Bel Air, designed and built by Envirotecture.

Fireproof asphalt shingles in a free-form wave pattern.

A north window and an unusual door. The interior is sheathed in cedar 2 × 8s.

Beveled glass and a carved handle make this door a pleasure to pass through.

This high-profile, 3v, elliptical frame is 30 feet higher than the deck. The 3 × 4 fir struts are from 5 to 8 feet long.

Concrete columns and pentagonal timber foundation on a steep hillside site. No grading required!

Arline Goldberg and Jerry Saltzman chose to take an owner-builder approach to their high-rise ellipse dome, using the talents of a number of dome builders along the way. The house was designed by Carey Smoot, and the work was done under the direction of Arline Goldberg and George Madarasz of Dome West. The tasty cabinetry was by John Crowley, inlaid steps by Chris Voorhees, and triangular doors by George Hoover. Virgil Smith and George Madarasz collaborated on the window details; Virgil should have special credit for his demanding standards and thoughtfulness. He installed 2 × 6 redwood frames over the 3 × 4 struts, but wanted to protect all the wood from the elements.

Using two flats, one angle, and four special bends, we were able to put together a system of fixed windows that can be opened and are both wind- and waterproof. We chose the hardware from one of the naval yards in Los Angeles. They're all brass with knurled knobs, a pleasure to handle.

The dayroom on the lower level under the deck.

The screened dayroom on the lower level. The pathways are of creek stone.

A window detail.

The Hooker home was built by Envirotecture in Topanga, California, in 1973. It has a tetrahedral truss frame with a 4 frequency elliptical dome that's 32 feet in diameter with an area of 800 square feet.

Inset: *A view from the south.*

These 3 × 4 struts are joined together with a pipe and strap hub system.

Above: *The entry bridge is attached to a suspended cantilevered deck. You leave the ground to "board" the ship!*

Left: *This system was pioneered by Bob Easton in Santa Barbara, California. There's minimal contact with the hillside, so no grading is needed.*

The kitchen/living area is divided by the bar. The only source of heat is the Ashley stove.

Ray Keller made these bathroom cabinets of old fir with square walnut pegs and pine panels. The vent pipe was left exposed.

Notice the turned struts of the top pentagon. The sheathing is 1 × 8 redwood.

The master suite. A spiral staircase leads to the dome above. The truss members on the interior are left exposed.

A fifty-foot full oblate spheroid (2v with 14" hub and 6 × 8 struts on the lower hemisphere and
4 × 8 struts on the upper) with windows of smoked Plexiglas and eleven pie-shaped decks inside. Completing this ship took several years out of Alan Hart and Robert Good's lives.

Alan Hart standing on struts ten feet away from the two-story spiraling floor levels. The interior structure was built first so it could be used as scaffolding.

Robin Daniel's home in the Malibu Mountains.

A lightweight plywood and foam dome (2 × 4 struts, 26' diameter) built by Jeff Fernald in Encinitas, California.

A double canvas skin dome (40' diameter, 4v elliptical) designed by Peter Calthorpe.

An unsuccessful ferrocement structure in the Malibu Mountains.

This small wood-shingle dome was designed and built by Dome West for Anna Marie Bernstrom, director of the Shram, a health and mind retreat in the Calabasas Hills. Intended solely for meditation, the space is undivided and represents a three- dimensional mandala.

Student housing at the University of California, Davis.

Dome West built this forty-foot cement geodesic dome for Jack Hill in Glenside. While we have a lot of reservations about the methods of texturing this medium, the realities of the future suggest that the lovely wooden structures we all love so well will be harder to find. And the monolithic shell quality of the ferrocement solves most of the sealing problems at the dihedrals in geodesics.

The inside of the same dome—it's being used as a laundromat.

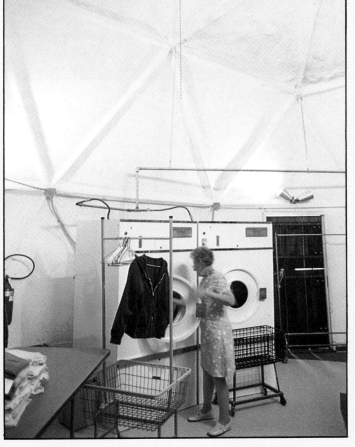

This twenty-foot-diameter tent (2 × 4 struts, ⅝ icosa, 3v) uses canvas that's water and fire resistant.

Two forms of portable shelter.

Below: *A tie-died tent dome made by students at the University of California, Davis.*

Above: *This tent dome built over a metal frame should last for about five to seven years. It has a ten-ounce water and fire resistant skin.*

Below: *A dome anchoring made of three-quarter-inch bolts run through a hub and a main floor beam.*

Above: *This four-dome residence in San Diego County is made of wood, with a foam skin.*

Right: *The inside of the seventy-foot-diameter oblate spheroid built by Bob Easton and Peter Calthorpe at the International Design Conference in Aspen, Colorado.*

The Krishnamurti Pavilion in Ojai, California. We were asked to build this nonreligious temple without relying on any particular architectural style. The important things were that the building last a hundred years, that it could be used for many purposes, and that when entering the main space a person would lose a sense of self.

The roof is made of cedar shingles, steamed and fitted to achieve the illusion of motion. They're also very durable. All the exterior nails in the roof and on the siding are made of copper. The stone is gray, the pine siding will turn gray as it ages—and the copper nails will bleed green. The shingles will turn gray too, blending in with the bark of the surrounding oak trees.

The Handelman house in the Malibu Mountains is a two-story wooden barn. On the lower level are stalls, tack and feed rooms, barn space, an art studio, and a spa with Jacuzzi and sauna. On the upper level, the kitchen, living, dining, and bath areas are all arranged in an open, semicircular plan, with a separate sleeping space. The roofing, roof deck, floors, and some of the interior walls are made of recycled materials.

The Handelman guest house, also called the "hypar cabin" because of the asymmetrical hyperbolic paraboloid roof system that curves in two different directions at the same time. The cabin has a sleeping loft with a kitchen below, all incorporated into a 14 by 20 foot floor plan.

Chapter 3. Property and Materials

CHOOSING YOUR PROPERTY

There are many things to take into consideration when choosing the site for your dome. The more carefully you plan, the fewer mistakes you'll make and the happier you'll be. Careful thought about your wants and needs—and the compromises you'll have to make along the way—is the key to a successful building project. Remember too that whatever type of dome you build and wherever you choose to build it, it should be built for positive reasons, with a positive spirit.

Even before you start to think about the site itself, consider its general geographic location. There are advantages and disadvantages inherent in any locale, be it rural, urban, or suburban. Personal taste always has a lot to do with these decisions, but it might not be a bad idea to talk to people who live in different settings, have moved from one to another, and have thought about the ways different environments have affected them.

Once you've decided on the general area that suits your interests, you should narrow your scope even further. Although neighborhoods may not be changing, the surrounding areas could be, and sooner or later you'll be affected. Investigate the neighborhood's history. Have there been large turnovers of real estate in short periods of time? Any changes will have a direct effect on the value of your property, no matter what you build on it or put into it. Check to see if local officials and realtors will provide information about tentative construction, industrial or otherwise.

You should also meet as many people in a neighborhood as you can. If you have difficulties with building codes and zoning regulations, this may just be an expression of the community's views on nonconformity. Society is generally slow to accept innovation, and many people still think domes are pretty unorthodox. Winning a decision from a local board of variance will not win over your future neighbors, but a casual conversation here and there may help them to become more familiar with domes.

SITE CONSIDERATIONS

The next step in your planning involves the site itself. Each building site has unique characteristics as distinct and subtle as a human personality. Get to know your land well, and build *with* it. If it's possible, try to see your land as it changes with the seasons and varying weather conditions. Notice its appearance on good days as well as bad. It's possible for a poor piece of real estate to look exceptionally good on a perfect day, but on the worst of days some of the qualities of a better piece of land will still manage to show through.

It's important to know the exact boundaries and the lay of the land since property lines and vertical elevations are critical. This information is available through the title company or the seller, and is included as a map in a title insurance policy. City or county building departments also have this information, or, if all else fails, you can order a plot map of your property prepared by a surveyor.

If your site doesn't slope too much in any direction, you might wish to determine its level yourself. One simple and fairly accurate method uses an ordinary garden hose. Choose what looks like the highest point of elevation on your site. After filling the hose with water, have one person hold each end vertically. While one person stands on the highest point, have the other walk downhill, keeping the water level even at both ends of the hose. Measuring the distance from both ends of the hose to the ground will give you the relative difference in elevation.

You should also investigate the qualities and characteristics of the soil. Sandy soil is porous, consisting of comparatively large grains, so it doesn't retain moisture very well. On the other hand, as the grains become smaller, the soil becomes more claylike and retains more moisture. This kind of soil has greater stability. You should remember that granular density influences stability, and stable foundations are essential to any form of construction.

If fill is used on your building site, see that it's been properly compacted. If not, it must be removed and replaced or else the foundation footings will have to penetrate the fill to the natural grade below.

Both the soil and the slope of your land will influence the way water drains from the site. If your plot is rough, hilly, or rests at a low point, drainage may be a problem. Many building codes require that the first floor be six inches above the level of the curb to prevent flooding.

Nature can contribute freely to your comfort in many ways, but one of its most important benefits is sunlight. Take note of the sun's path across your property during all the seasons—it plays an important part in whether or not your dome is well lighted, and of course it's vital if you have solar heating in mind.

Think of your daily activities and where you're apt to be spending your time at certain parts of the day. Morning activities centering around the bathroom and kitchen areas mean they should be located where the rising eastern sun can reach them. Following the sun as the day continues, more direct light may fall on a general living area, while at dinner time you might want a view of the western sun. But don't forget about darkness either. The subtle influences of shading are important in designing a dome. And remember that as the seasons change, the sun will reach your dome at different angles.

It's a good idea to keep the prevailing wind direction in mind too—proper ventilation is an important part of an efficient dome design. As a blast of wind hits the structure it creates an area of high pressure on the outside. You can take advantage of this by placing a large ventilator at the point of high pressure and an even larger one on the other side of the dome, where there's contrasting low pressure. The low pressure side can be suited with a vent that takes advantage of the suction caused by this type of air flow around a building. This can be a very efficient form of natural ventilation.

The view from your dome will probably come to mean a great deal to you. Generally it's a good idea to leave as much of the natural surroundings as possible untouched. Even shrubbery that at first has no apparent value may reveal a useful purpose that you couldn't have foreseen. It's best not to tear down any trees without careful consideration. Trees often take lifetimes to reach maturity, they provide shade, and are a natural buffer against all kinds of weather. If you *must* remove a tree from your property, go about it wisely. It can be an expensive proposition, so if you have the ability, take the tree down yourself and recycle the wood. If there's a lumber mill in the area, you might want to have the wood milled. It can be rough cut; cut and dressed; or cut, dressed, and treated—whatever is needed in your building project. Or you could always sell it. If you're not so ambitious, the wood from your tree can be cut, quartered, and used for firewood. Depending on your skills as a woodcutter and the quantity and quality of wood you have, you may be able to split rails and put up some fencing. The point to remember is that the uses of wood around your building site are virtually limitless.

Keep in mind the fact that you may want to view some play or work areas from inside the dome. If you plan a vegetable garden or flower bed, you ought to be able to enjoy them from within as well as without.

One way to get an idea of the overall view of your site is through photography. Take some shots in every direction—this may clarify which views you prefer and show the effects of the surrounding scenery more clearly. It's also good to think about the view of your site from the outside in, since that's how other people will see your dome.

Get to know your utilities people, too. Find out about sewer lines, and water, electrical, and power services. If your dome will need these services you'll have to know where they're located. When you're ready to have them connected, the utility companies will discuss the method involved with you. But for the purpose of planning your dome, all you really need to know is how and where the separate services enter your property. This will enable you to anticipate any difficulties the use of various utilities may impose, and give you time to devise solutions to the problems.

Once all of your planning is completed, you should have a fair idea of how your dome will look on your property, nestled within the surrounding scenery. Picture how it will change the site, and visualize your project both as an image in a sweeping panorama and as a focal point in the foreground. The clearer this picture is, the better you'll know your site and scenery and the more familiar you'll be with your dome before you've even begun to build.

Photography may be a help to you here as well. You may know of a dome similar to the one you're planning. Try taking a picture of it and superimposing it on a shot of your proposed building site. You might be able to piece together a picture of what your home will look like even before you've started working on it.

Many professionals construct models for every dome they build, and you'd be wise to follow their example. Building a model will help you become familiar with curvilinear structure, geometrics, and the patterns developed through geodesic design. In the process of building a model dome, mathematical theorems are transformed from abstractions to concrete reality—and detailed models will help you isolate potential problem areas. Aside from being a practical aid, model building can also be a lot of fun. Consult John Prenis' *The Dome Builder's Handbook* for more information.

FOUNDATIONS

This section and the sections that follow deal with the general techniques and principles involved in building a dome. My aim is to illustrate the process rather than give you specific instructions. This book isn't a step-by-step manual; instead, it will give you an overview and help you understand exactly what building a dome will entail. From this, you should be able to tell whether or not you'll need outside help with any particular parts of the project.

Continuous Wall Foundations

Continuous wall foundations are made of concrete blocks or poured concrete. Unless you've had experience with blocks, it isn't a good idea to begin learning while building a foundation for your home. It *does* require some skill. For more information on block foundations, check the next chapter.

If you're going to attempt your own foundation, poured concrete may be the safest way to go. The following description of the process will give you an idea of what's involved. If you decide on this method, you'll find *The Mechanix Illustrated How-To-Do-It Encyclopedia* or Charles Neal's *Do-It-Yourself House Building Step-by-Step* helpful references.

Footings are the first step. The specific width and depth will probably be precisely determined by local building codes. The outside perimeter should

be completely staked out and the ground leveled. Then 2 X 6's and 2 X 8's are placed on edge to serve as retaining walls for the poured concrete. Stakes are driven into the ground and nailed to the boards to secure them. Ten- penny nails and a lot of stakes provide support against the pressure of the heavy concrete. The footing forms are then leveled.

The ground where the concrete will be poured is checked to be sure it's level and square, and if more dirt has to be excavated, it's used for bracing and packed along the outside of the footing forms. At this point, yet another bracing system is used against the pressure of the concrete—scrap lumber is nailed across the tops of the footing forms at ten-foot intervals. The scraps are longer than the width of the footings and are often referred to as "cats."

Next comes the pouring of the concrete, which should have a thick consistency. The looser the mix, the weaker it is. The concrete is poured between the footing forms and is then shovelled along until the forms are full. Just before the concrete has hardened, the braces across the tops of the forms are temporarily removed so that lengths of 2 X 4's can be sunk into the center of the footings. This creates a keyway, adding to the strength of the foundation wall that rests on top. The concrete is then leveled. This is done roughly, not with a trowel—it's easier for the fresh concrete to bond to a rough surface. The following day, both the footing forms and the center 2 X 4 keys are removed, scraped clean, and saved. The footing is then completed.

The foundation walls themselves are made next, and the forms used in this process have the same purpose as those used for the footings. They can be sheets of plywood with vertically nailed and evenly spaced 2 X 4's as uprights. The two outside 2 X 4's are flush to the edges of the plywood so a continuous wall can be formed by nailing them together.

When the footing is swept clean, a chalk line is snapped to indicate the position of the outside walls. These walls are then set in place, nailed top and bottom, and braced along the outside to hold them upright. Although the line formed is somewhat crooked it is later straightened by the addition of boards called "walers" which span the length of the walls. Metal rods are inserted through predrilled holes in the plywood panels to guard against the pressure exerted by the poured concrete. The rods are secured by spreader washers on the inside and by wedges on the outside of the walers.

The inside walls are set up like the outside ones— the metal rods are put in place and the walers are secured on both the inside and outside walls. The forms must be perpendicular and are checked with a

level. If they need to be adjusted, this is done carefully with a sledge hammer or a house jack if necessary. A strip is added—also level—which marks the top of the foundation wall and is used as a guide during the pour. Where a beam is to nest in a part of the wall, a box is nailed to the form and the concrete is molded around it.

Bracing is crucial when you're pouring concrete. Stakes are driven near the base of the footing, and braces are run from these to the base of the foundation wall. Similar stakes are driven at ground level, and braces are run to the wall above the top level of walers. Diagonal braces run from the ground to the wall on both sides of the foundation wall.

The concrete is poured from the corners, and the bottom two feet are allowed to begin setting before the rest of the pour is made. As it's being poured, a long length of 2 X 4 is periodically used to tamp the concrete. This prevents the concrete from setting against the sides of the forms in pockets. The level of concrete is always brought up a little at a time and as evenly as possible around all sides of the foundation forms because of the great stress it exerts. The trick is to get an even distribution of that stress.

The concrete foundation walls are allowed to dry for about two days before the walers are removed. A day or so after this, the foundation wall forms can be stripped away from the walls themselves. The metal tie rods protruding from the walls can then be snapped off and the holes that remain are filled with Portland cement and sand.

Next the exterior walls are waterproofed with an asphalt-based compound that is either brushed or troweled on depending on its consistency. The base is coated most heavily, but the top of the footing is coated as well. Two coats are usually applied. Finally the foundation is carefully backfilled.

Pile Foundations

Pile foundations are formed by sinking long con-

crete columns or treated wood posts into the ground until bedrock or a hard layer of soil is reached, or until they can support a certain load. This is a deeper form of foundation than most traditional systems, and it's often used when surface soil conditions make continuous wall foundations unsafe. For example, softer soils may be incapable of withstanding the load of a completed home. If a foundation settles too much it will crack, and could make the completed house unsafe.

When a pile foundation is being considered, soil conditions should be studied carefully. If a firm layer of soil lies on top of a soft layer, it's probably better to lay a more traditional foundation. The firm layer of soil will act as a natural pad for a traditional system while posts driven through a hard layer may break it up and result in an exceptionally weak and unstable foundation.

Post foundations haven't been widely used in this country in spite of their advantages. This could be due to resistance from contractors, who may claim, among other reasons, that connecting beams require special attachments or that electrical wiring is difficult. For them, the disadvantages outweigh the advantages. However, when properly constructed, post foundations are much stronger than more con-

ventional ones.

If wood posts are used, they must be treated with preservative in order to protect against bugs, rot, and decay. Creosote is very effective for this since it can be forced into timber by vacuum and pressure processes, ensuring maximum penetration. It can also be applied manually. Whatever treatment process you decide on, penetration should equal at least half the radius of the post.

In some cases, a footing for pole-type foundations may not be required. This depends on the capacities of the soil, and since the structure involved is a permanent dwelling, careful thought should be given to this consideration. The point where the pole rests against the soil determines each post's exact load-bearing capacity, and only where the soil is very dense should a pole foundation without footings be considered. Uneven settling could cause serious trouble later on.

Holes for post foundations can be dug with a post hole digger. The manually operated kind will work fairly well in most soils—if you don't mind time-consuming, sometimes difficult, work. Sears sells a selection of gasoline-powered post hole diggers for between two and three hundred dollars, as well as augers of various lengths and diameters. Post hole diggers can also be rented. An industrial equipment supplier in my area was able to supply an auger-type post hole digger mounted on the back of a jeep for forty dollars a day.

The exact depth of the posts will be determined by the frost line. The holes should be dug to the size of the footings desired—in other words, wider than the foundation post. In softer soil, a larger footing is required; you also need a larger footing when the distance between foundation posts increases. Dirt shouldn't be left too near the holes, and loose dirt should be removed from the holes before the footings are poured.

A base line is laid out so that a level string and stake system will show the height of the beams on which the platform will be built. The lengths of the individual posts are then determined by measuring from each footing to the height of the string. In some post and beam foundations, the top of the posts are notched and prepared to fit with your plans before they are sunk. They should be loosely held in position with eight to ten inches of dirt and each post checked against the plans. Only then should the holes be completely filled in. Once everything has been checked, the holes should be filled slowly about six inches at a time, and each level of fill should be solidly tamped to ensure a sturdy foundation. You might also consider using gravel, broken stone, or some concrete in the holes for added strength. If the posts are to extend any appreciable distance above ground, they should be sufficiently crossbraced.

Concrete piles can either be precast or cast in place. Precast piles are reinforced in order to withstand the stresses of handling, and they're extremely heavy. This is one of the factors limiting their use. Another factor is the difficulty in cutting if they prove too long—and the difficulty in increasing their length if they're too short.

The most widely used form of concrete pile is the cast-in-place pile in which concrete is poured directly into the ground. There are two forms of cast-in-place piles. Concrete poured directly into the hole and directly touching the soil forms an uncased pile. A cased pile is formed when concrete is poured into a tube that is dropped or driven into the ground and serves as a form.

THE TWO MAIN KINDS OF DOMES

The two types of dome houses generally available today are classified by their method of construction—frame and skin or panel. In frame and skin domes, a triangular framework is erected, usually of 2 X 4's, 2 X 6's, or 2 X 8's. These components are called struts. The triangles are held together at the vertices by connecting hardware known as hubs. These vary according to the manufacturer's designs, and are usually made of steel or aluminum. In most cases, the skin that covers the triangular sections is either half-inch plywood or some form of composition-chip panel board. The skin is nailed and glued in place.

Panel domes generally use the same materials, but their method of construction does away with the hub system. Prefabricated triangular components are joined, usually with a nut and bolt system, to form the pentagons and hexagons that make up the dome. Then they're hoisted in place—sometimes with the aid of machinery— and bolted together to form the completed shell. Unlike frame and skin domes, in which the hubs provide for the angles, bevel cuts on the component edges serve that purpose in panel domes. Though panel domes use a bit more material and are generally a little more expensive than frame and skin domes, they're easier to put together and can be constructed more quickly.

Most of the mathematics of dome building has been taken care of by manufacturers through precutting and color coding struts, hubs, and panels. Manufactured panels with beveled edges provide for dehedral angles (the angles between triangles) as well as face angles (the angles at the tips of skin

panels). If they're put together in the proper order, the components will go together fairly easily. But when the only manufactured component you're buying is a connector kit, you'll need to have a clear understanding of chord factors.

Chord factors are calculated from central angles by means of a formula and are used in determining the lengths of struts. In other words, strut length equals the dome's radius multiplied by the appropriate chord factor. *The Dome Builder's Handbook, Domenotes*, and *Shelter* provide plenty of information on chord factors. Several other helpful books are either out of print or very difficult to find, but they're worth the effort if you can locate them— Lloyd Kahn's *Domebook 2, Dome Cookbook of Geodesic Geometry* by David Kruschki, *Dome Cookbook* by Steve Baer, and *Geodesics* by Edward Popko.

WINDOWS

There are six basic styles of conventional windows. Most of us are familiar with the double hung window with upper and lower sashes that slide vertically within separate grooves or weather stripping. The maximum opening a double hung window can provide is one half the total window space.

Picture windows are also fairly common. These fixed windows usually consist of a large sheet of insulated glass set permanently into a frame. They may be installed with or without a sash, and they generally don't open and close.

Awning and hopper windows are similar in nature since they both have one opening sash. Awning windows are hinged at the top and swing out at the bottom, while hopper windows are hinged at the bottom and swing in from the top.

Casement windows are very much like awning and hopper windows. These are hinged along one side and can swing in or out, though they're usually designed to swing out because this style is easier to make weathertight. The advantage of casement windows is that they can provide more ventilation when completely open, since the total window area is unobstructed.

Finally, there are windows that slide back and forth on separate horizontal tracks located on the head jamb and window sill.

Assuring weathertight window systems has always been a problem with dome homes. Installing windows in a curved surface is tricky to begin with, and the greater amount of expansion and contraction in domes just makes it all more complicated. Most dome kit manufacturers have solved water leakage and other window sealing problems by adapting their designs to include dormers and riser walls. A dormer system projects out from the surface of the dome and produces a vertical surface so that any standard window system can be installed. Riser walls also serve the same purpose. By using these solutions to the window sealing problem in domes, manufacturers can offer a great variety of window designs to their customers, and most seem to handle the whole matter fairly well.

Triangular windows—those that don't use dormers or any other design adaptations that break the dome's geometric symmetry—are much more complex. Custom builders have developed weathertight systems for these kinds of windows, but often at considerable expense. To get an idea of how these systems work, have a look at the color photos of the Saltzman-Goldberg dome. Then check them against the window details in the blueprint section.

MATERIALS

Usually standard wood building materials are used by commercial manufacturers. However, a few use plastics in manufacturing components. In either case, you should be familiar with the advantages and disadvantages of each kind of material.

Wood

Wood is a popular building material for practical as well as aesthetic reasons. Although the price of wood is going up, it's still comparatively inexpensive. Of course, there are many other reasons why people prefer wood as a building material.

Wood is one of the oldest building materials. Over thousands of years it's been used in many different ways, and new ones are still being found to-

day. Most recently, advanced cutting and milling techniques have resulted in plywoods that are thin veneers glued together with their grains running perpendicular at adjoining layers. The advent of adhesives has also made it possible to produce particle boards from wood chips and pulp.

There are two basic types of wood, hardwood and softwood. The softwoods are generally from the evergreen family, while hardwoods are leaf-bearing. Hardwood is generally more dense and durable; it's used for flooring and furniture because it's strong and doesn't give as readily as softwood. Sculptors are fond of hardwood because it lends itself to delicate work.

But while hardwoods offer better quality, a wider choice of color, and more potential for fine craftsmanship, they're usually more expensive, and building an entire house from them is far from economical. Besides, the less expensive softwoods have an advantage in that they *do* give. They're easier to cut and generally easier to work with. They can withstand more sawing, notching, and cutting before they'll split and crack.

Usually all wood used for construction is seasoned lumber. Seasoning refers to a drying process that eliminates moisture, a prime factor in the shrinking, swelling, and warping of wood. Seasoning also increases the strength of wood and gives it a higher degree of resistance to decay. Timber seasoned through natural exposure to the air is referred to as air dried, while lumber seasoned through more accelerated and controlled processes is referred to as kiln dried. Very often the drying process is marked on the purchased lumber. Air drying takes about two to six months, depending on the location, the humidity, the type of wood being treated, and the size of the lumber.

Lumber must be properly stacked so that air can circulate fully through it, otherwise it will take longer to dry and there may also be some decay. Kiln drying is more satisfactory, but care must be taken in this process as well. Temperatures that are too high may result in split, warped, and "checked" lumber (a lengthwise separation in the grain). These flaws occur when there's too great a disparity between the dry outside and moist inside areas of the wood. On the other hand, temperatures that are too low may allow the growth of fungus on wood that is warm and moist.

Natural air drying cuts the wood's shrinkage in half; about two-thirds of the shrinkage factor is removed through kiln drying.

Lumber that has not been seasoned is known as "green" lumber. Although it's highly subject to shrinkage, it's also substantially cheaper than seasoned lumber. In some cases, green lumber can be used in place of seasoned timber if it's allowed to season at the completion of a construction phase before further work is done. Of course, in building that requires precision, shrinkage variables prohibit the use of green lumber.

"Dressing" is the part of the milling process that makes the lumber's dimensions more exact. Although in its rough state a 2 X 4 is actually 2 inches thick and 4 inches wide, when it's dressed it's more like 1½ inches thick and 3½ inches wide. Dressed lumber does not weather as well as rough lumber, and rough lumber is always stronger.

Plywood, a practical and very widely used wood product, is known for its stress capabilities, resistance to moisture, and overall integrity as a building material. Plywood is made by gluing and pressing together thin sheets of wood to form a panel. The exposed face of this panel is known as the face veneer, the hidden side as the back veneer, and the interior as the core.

Plywood usually comes in standard widths, while lengths start at five feet and increase by one foot intervals up to twelve feet. The most common dimension, 4 X 8 feet, is thought of as the standard sheet of plywood.

The thickness of plywood is determined by the number of plies, and the face plies are usually a bit thinner than the core plies. A single ply is usually 1/8 inch thick, but sometimes they can be as thin as 1/16 inch. The grain of the front and back plies normally runs parallel to the long side of the panel, and since plies are glued perpendicular to each other, the finished piece is made with an odd number of plies.

Plywood is classified very broadly as either interior or exterior plywood. Interior plywood is bonded with moisture resistant protein glue, the intermediate glue used for exterior plywood is much more resistant to moisture, decay, bacteria, and mold. Sometimes interior plywood is subject to excessive moisture, and in that case exterior glue can be substituted. The glues used in exterior grades of plywood are designed to withstand water penetration and cycles of moisture and dryness.

Seasoning is the easiest way to prevent most woods from decaying, but moisture can cause seasoning to lose its effectiveness. The best way to combat this is by using preservatives that penetrate the wood and poison fungi. The most practical wood preservative is creosote, or a creosote solution. Either one can be brushed or sprayed on; dipping gives an even higher penetration.

Plastics

There's been quite a bit of negative talk about plastics over the past few years. Many plastics chip, scratch, or crack; they're costly to manufacture and difficult to work with; they give off poisonous gases when they burn and don't biodegrade like wood. However, there are some areas where plastics perform very well.

Waterproofing is one of these areas. Polysulfide, silicone, and acrylic sealants function well even under severe conditions such as large shifts in window frames and structural movement. Some sealants are very stiff when cured, while "live" sealants are more resilient. Convex, domed plastic skylights minimize leakage and double domed skylights cut down on heat loss and solve condensation problems.

The adhesives we rely on for strength and durability are based on plastics. Laminated timber, waterproof plywood, and wood particle chipboards are all held together with polymeric adhesives. And then there are plastic partitions, which can be lightweight, hollow, and filled with foam or other soundproofing materials.

Plastics come in a wide range of colors and can be molded into virtually any shape imaginable. In many cases, plastic can be used interchangeably with metal parts like knobs, handles, latches, and gears. Plastics are also available in a variety of textures and can either reflect or diffuse light. They can be exceptionally tough and durable and can lend these qualities to other building materials. For example, when latex or epoxy is added to stucco, it greatly increases the stucco's strength and bonding capacity.

Since all these plastics are a comparatively new addition to the building industry, the processes for their manufacture are still somewhat complex, and in many cases their application to contemporary dwellings requires the knowledge and expertise of qualified professionals.

On a basic level, a plastic may be defined as a material that possesses carbon, an organic element. At some stage of its manufacture it's shaped into various forms, usually through the application of heat and/or pressure, and emerges in its finished state as a solid. The carbon used in the manufacture of plastic is present in the form of resins. These can be natural, but they're usually synthetic. Synthetic resins come from the chemical processing of materials like coal, petroleum, natural gas, water, salt, and air. Different types of resins are used in different types of plastic according to their physical and chemical makeup. Other substances are also added: plasticizers affect flexibility, fillers—powdered quartz, slate, clay, mica, and asbestos fibers—improve certain qualities like flexibility and strength, and colorants account for the great range of shades in which plastic is available.

There are two classifications of plastics based on their behavior as they are heated and cooled in the manufacturing process. Thermoplastics are softened by a heat process, and as they solidify and cool they regain their original properties. Chemical changes don't occur, and the process can be repeated again and again. On the other hand, a chemical change *does* take place in the manufacture of thermosetting plastics. As the name implies, these take a set, solidify while they're still hot, and the process cannot be performed again.

The thermosetting plastics often used in dome building, polystyrene and polyurethane foam, are produced through the addition of an expanding agent. This causes the material to form cells, increasing the material's original volume many times.

In building a dome with plastic, certain practical, economic considerations must be taken into account. Although domes cover the greatest space with the least possible material, the extensive use of plastic will still be impractical in most cases. The costs of traditional building materials are steadily increasing, but still the expense of plastic exceeds them. More and more kinds of plastic are appearing in greater and greater quantities, but the ideal plastic that's highly durable, has the visual quality of glass, and is inexpensive has not yet been invented.

Many plastics can become discolored through exposure to the sun. In general they just don't seem to have the qualities that enable more natural building materials to weather well and age gracefully. Constant handling can scratch, soil, and discolor many plastics. In contrast, wood that's constantly handled will develop a rich luster from the natural oils of the skin. Some plastics—foam, for example—can easily be gouged and nicked even when protected with a hard surface, and this adds to the expense of their use.

There's one hazard with polyurethane foam that can't be overlooked—fire. Polyurethane foam doesn't catch fire easily, but once it does it burns furiously in spite of its fire retardant additives. Once ignited, foam can go up in seconds and burns like gasoline, producing the poisonous di-isocyanate gases from which it was manufactured.

Despite this, foams are still some of the best insulators around. When properly applied, they do a fine job—and they're being improved all the time.

Chapter 4. Some Basics of Dome Building

For the past five years, Howard Johnson and his family have lived in a dome on the coast of Maine. Howard built the dome himself, and before that he spent a year studying house designs and building models. Howard is now an architect specializing in low-cost domes. His firm, Domaine, is involved in both consulting and building. Howard Johnson believes the research stage is crucial to the success of any dome project. Anyone who's thinking about putting up a dome home should read everything they can find on building techniques for both conventional and unconventional houses and talk to experienced builders. Poor planning, poor construction techniques, and a general failure to do the right homework are some reasons for the faulty results that have sometimes given owner-built domes a bad name.

Howard Johnson's low-cost, comfortable, and permanent dome was built using a combination of conventional building techniques and the knowledge gained from studying and experimenting with dome building. He has a lot of valuable advice for dome builders, and agreed to tape record some of it for this book. The entries that follow are based on his tapes. Some of Howard's recommendations are best suited to Maine's cold climate, but most of his techniques will be of interest to dome builders everywhere.

FOUNDATIONS

Block foundations are perfectly adequate, and by laying your own it's possible to save up to a dollar a block in labor. The footing should be put down below the frost line so the frost won't move the foundations or crack them. Block foundations are also good because no forms are needed and corners (there are twelve in our foundations) are easy to make.

The footing is laid first. In our dome it's 8 inches deep and 16 inches wide and contains reinforcing rod all the way around. We used 2 X 10's as forms for the concrete pour and 1 X 3 strapping (spreaders) to hold the 2 X 10's in place. Sometimes a keyway is put in by placing 2 X 4 lengthwise into the center of the footing's upper surface. Techniques for this can be found in any conventional building book. A transit, used for leveling, costs about a hundred dollars and is well worth the price—or borrow or rent one from someone who isn't using theirs.

When the footing has dried, it's time to provide for drainage. A piece of plastic pipe is laid in the clay—it's black, flexible, and has slits in it. The pipe goes all the way around the foundation, underground and away from the building, down a hill or into a storm sewer. Generally, tar paper is put on top of it. Then three feet of clean gravel is put on top of the tar paper, and the upper foot is filled with dirt. Water penetrates the layer of gravel, then washes through the drain pipe and away from the house.

After this, the wall is built on top of the foundation. If the building is being done on top of ledge rock, holes are drilled down into the ledge with a star drill or a jack hammer. Reinforcing bars are then put into the holes. They stick up, and you can fasten the framework directly to them. If part of the house is going to be on a ledge and part on mud, the foundation is floated above the ledge rock to compensate for the uneven settling that sometimes makes a foundation crack.

Another foundation that works very well is a system of concrete piles. It's well integrated and very inexpensive. Banks may not like it because they prefer to have a solid foundation underneath every building, but it *is* one of the cheapest foundation systems around. You should consult a conventional building text for the spacing of the support beams for floors since a concrete pile must be placed beneath each one of these posts. Holes are then dug for the outside piles as well as for the poles that support the outside load. Heavy-gauge cardboard tubing—available in 6, 8, 10, or 12 inch diameters and whatever pile thickness necessary—is dropped right in the holes. Dirt is backfilled into the holes and adequately packed. Then concrete is simply poured into the tubes.

If the soil is not sufficiently dense and more support is necessary, larger holes may have to be dug so that concrete pads can be poured in the bottom of the pile holes. Then the tube is placed on top of this pad. You can also build 2 X 4's right into the tubes, and insulation board can be nailed directly onto these 2 X 4's to form the outside of the house.

The piles should go down at least 4 feet to make sure they're below the frost line. If you don't, the ground freezes, expands, catches on the wall, and raises the wall with it. When you're ready to pour the concrete, nails are poked through the tubes at the correct height, using a transit, and the concrete is then poured to this level.

Next, trusses are built from 2 X 4's. You'll need a lot of 2 X 4's and half-inch CDX plywood, along with a good circular saw. Speaking of tools in general, it's

78

best to have a few good ones and take care of them rather than be stuck with many neglected and inferior tools. Remember to buy enough blades for your saw so you always have sharp ones on hand.

The truss system is determined by the area to be spanned—a truss system 20 inches tall will span a 20-foot distance. The truss system in our dome uses the 2:4:1 method in which trusses are 4 feet apart. A radial arm saw helps in making the many repetitive cuts; use a cleat so that every piece is the same length. Sears sells a good one for $250. Wait for a sale.

When the trusses are up, insulation board is nailed below them. If you can't buy it thick enough to span the 4 feet without sagging, you can use 2 X 4's to keep it from warping. The seams are then sealed all the way around with duct tape. On top of this, 8 or 9 inches of insulation is installed. Finally, the 1 1/8 inch plywood tongue-and-groove floor is glued and nailed in place. This provides about 12 inches of dead air space that's essential to the heating and cooling system, since it provides room to circulate air at various temperatures throughout different parts of the house. The edges of the floor are capped off with boards; these don't quite reach the edge of the dome, which provides air passage. Insulation board is put up around the outside of the

dome to prevent air from blowing underneath. Styrofoam insulation is put on the inside of these walls.

This foundation system is inexpensive because there are no costly stud walls, the cement is in the piles, the floor is made of inexpensive materials, the trusses can be of great length, and no heavy machinery is necessary. You're also guaranteed a dry house.

For further information on pole foundations, the U.S. Government Printing Office and the U.S. Forest Service in Madison, Wisconsin, can provide stacks of material at a very low price. They have information about using telephone poles for piles; they've been reported to last up to forty years.

STRUT, SKIN, AND PANEL CONSTRUCTION

Becoming familiar with different sizes and truncations of domes is all part of doing your homework in preparing for building. When you're considering different plans, making models helps you to see them as three-dimensional realities. The many different forms of domes, geometrics, and geodesic math have all been dealt with quite extensively, and by studying other texts, such as *The Dome Builder's Handbook* or *Domenotes,* you can become familiar with them. This is the only way terminology like 3V

5/8 icosahedral and 4V 1/2 octahedral will become clear.

Smaller domes—from 20 to 28 feet in diameter—can be constructed quickly by nailing together complete triangles of struts and plywood and then assembling the triangles into a completed dome. This method is slightly more expensive than the more common one that uses hubs, but it eliminates the need for these connector systems. The triangles can be assembled by driving eight-penny nails through the struts of the triangles and bending them over, a process known as clinch nailing. Nuts and bolts can also be used, but this is more expensive and time consuming, and as long as you don't plan on moving the dome, nuts and bolts aren't absolutely necessary.

A sheetrock gun will accomplish the same thing. It looks like a drill but has a magnetized Phillips head screwdriver point and a clutch so the sheetrock screws only penetrate to a set distance. Though more expensive than nails, sheetrock screws are less expensive than regular screws. They're self-tapping, so there's no need for predrilled holes. Just mount the screw on the sheetrock gun, hold it to the surface, and you'll have a secure joining of the triangles.

A 3V 5/8 alternate with a 9.8 foot radius has proved to be an inexpensive, ideal size for this building pro-

cess, and splicing several of these domes together can provide a very comfortable dwelling. You can also work in a loft system hung with chains. Inexpensive 1 X 3 strapping can be used for the struts. A quicker way to make struts is to buy #4 grade 1 X 8 lumber and rip it into two pieces exactly the same size at a 7 degree angle with a table or radial arm saw. This allows you to cut struts from 8-foot 1 X 3's or 16-foot 1 X 8's. You can use these to make four triangles from a single sheet of 4 X 8 CDX plywood three-eighths of an inch thick. The prefabbing process makes the total construction time a little longer, but the dome itself can be put up very quickly.

Unless you have a crane or an elaborate scaffolding and bracing system, prefab triangles won't work for large domes because they'll be too heavy and unwieldy to manage when the triangles begin curving inward. They must be supported until they're all together. This necessitates going to a strut and hub system and covering the frame with a skin. Plywood hubs are not advisable because of their tendency to rotate (known as turbining). This causes the triangular dimensions to change, and then each triangular section has to be custom cut, a very time-consuming process.

The best investment an economy-minded owner-builder can make is Bill Woods' Dyna Dome Con-

nector System. There are no bevel cuts, it's highly engineered, and the blueprints and instructions are all very clear. Also, the strut lengths and triangle sizes are such that there is very little waste.

For larger domes, staging on wheels is necessary. This can be moved around on the floor as people work from the top. The only problem is that most staging is about six or seven feet wide and the strut length on larger domes is about eight feet, so someone is usually dangling off one end of the staging. Masonry staging is about ten feet wide, and if it's available it will make everything easier.

Make a model of your dome and color code it to match the appropriate markings on your wooden struts. Having this model right on the floor of your dome will be a great help; many dome builders even require it. The models are used as a key when coded struts are passed up to workers on the staging. When all the struts are bolted in place, the dome becomes very rigid and the bolts can be tightened with hand wrenches or an electric impact wrench.

You can hoist the triangles into place by using a pully system mounted in the top of the dome with a rope that runs from the outside and dangles all the way down through the center. The rope can be attached to a large nail hammered into each triangle. The triangles are pulled into position and put in place by workers on the outside of the dome who are also safely supported by ropes.

The rough flooring of the dome provides an adequate work area for this process. To custom cut one triangular panel, first measure the three sides of the triangle. On a piece of wood, use a straight edge to draw the the longest side. Then take a tape measure and hold a pencil to one end while another person holds the other at the precise length of another side. Lay this down on the line representing the longest side. The person holding the tape should make sure it's still at the end of the first, longest line. Then simply draw an arc. Repeat this process on the opposite end of the line representing the longest side with the measurement of the third side. The two arcs intersect at the third point of the triangle. Then a chalk line can be snapped, producing the precise size of the triangle you need.

The same method can be used for covering the insides of the triangles, which have a different dimension. Using a chalk line wrapped around large nails driven into the subfloor at the points of the triangle, a line can be snapped onto tongue-and-groove boards which cover the triangular area. Then by pulling out the nails and setting a skill saw at the exact depth of the boards, you can saw the interior boards right as they are on the subfloor. With this

process, interior boards can either be marked and stacked or handed up to other workers who can put them directly in place. The boards should be cut fairly close to the measure, but they don't have to be exact because the edges can be covered with stripping.

SHINGLING

Improper shingling will result in leaks, and leaking has been one of the biggest problems in building domes. Particular care must be taken in order to do the job correctly. Cedar shingles and shakes, although much more aesthetically pleasing, are more difficult, expensive, and time consuming to work with than asphalt shingles.

Since they're irregular in shape, shakes are prone to leakage. This problem can be solved by using a 24-inch shake with an 8-inch exposure so that 16 inches of the shake will be covered. In this way, every place on the roof is covered by at least three thicknesses of shakes. It's sometimes difficult to assure this, though, because there are so many angles on a dome, and a lot of cutting is involved. Flashing must also be expertly installed.

All of this is not impossible, but it *is* very, very difficult. Unless you have a lot of experience with cedar shakes and shingles, you ought to hire an expert to work with you if you decide on one of these roofing

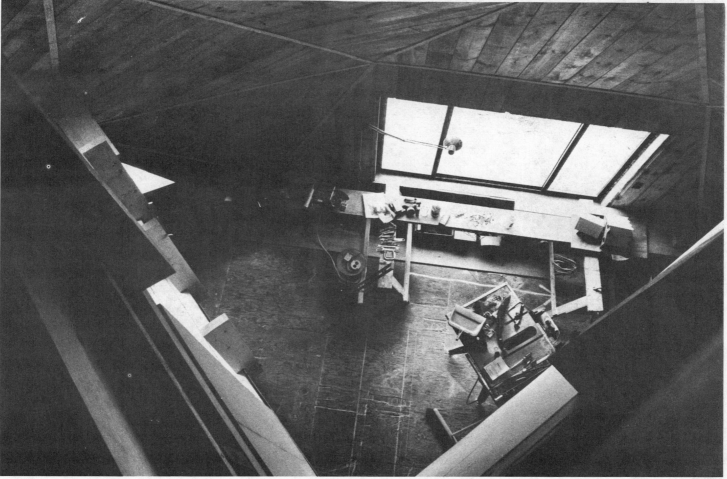

materials. In this way, you can learn the process as you go along, and the supervision will assure you of the quality work that's essential when constructing a watertight roof.

Conventional asphalt shingles are a more practical roofing material. They're also cheaper. Asphalt shingles (245 pounds) have a retail cost of about $22 a square (100 square feet) in Maine. Cedar shingles that are clear (free of knots) run about $35 a square, and shakes cost about $65 a square. There are different grades and types of shingles and shakes available; they can either be machine cut or hand split. Machine-cut shakes are easier to put on, but hand-split shakes are thicker and look better.

Chapter 5. Dome Manufacturers

The information in this chapter was gathered by writing to commercial dome home manufacturers. After sending each company a form letter and a questionnaire, we drew up a dome home owner's questionnaire and asked the manufacturers to distribute this among their clients. Although the response to the second questionnaire was minimal, we *did* receive some interesting letters.

The companies' responses to our inquiries varied. In some cases, correspondence was returned, and in others we discovered after several tries that the company's corporate status and ownership had changed. Some companies cooperated in part and some not at all; others were very helpful. This is a pretty good indication of the state of the dome home industry—if the kit manufacturing business were just a bit more firmly established, we probably would have come up with a lot more concrete information.

Some manufacturers' responses raised tricky questions. Pamphlets filled with sketches might suggest that the organization hadn't yet built any domes, or, worse, didn't wish to show any that they'd built. But even photographs can be deceiving, regardless of their quantity and quality. One picture may show foundation work, another a completed frame, and others various stages of the construction—all of the same single dome. This may not mean that the dome isn't a good one, just that the company may only have built that one dome.

Compared to housing construction as a whole, dome home building is pretty much a cottage industry. The first commercial dome kits were developed about twenty years ago, and the field, while still relatively small, is growing in size and acceptance. There's a lot of potential, but the direction commercial dome building takes in the future depends largely on the integrity of the individuals involved and the responsibilities they assume. Right now there are some good products on the market, and there's a lot of change and improvement going on. However, any new and growing industry is bound to attract some undesirable elements, and this is obviously a concern of both consumers and reputable manufacturers. Of course, domes should not be singled out for special attention; the same kinds of problems are found in conventional construction. You should be alert.

The dome home industry has a professional trade organization, the National Association of Dome Home Manufacturers, which is trying to set standards to promote a viable industry. This organization is open to all dome home manufacturers, builder-dealers, and suppliers, and accepts associate members who simply wish to be kept informed of developments.

Although the members of N.A.D.H.M. are competitors, they have more power as a group when dealing with matters like insurance, materials' costs, and financing. Because the commercially manufactured dome home is still new to most people, the association also strives to promote its acceptance as a viable housing form and increase public confidence in the various dome-home-building systems. The special nature of the dome structure sometimes creates difficulties with building and zoning officials, and N.A.D.H.M. is trying to change this situation. N.A.D.H.M. also familiarizes lending institutions with ways of financing dome homes.

Applications for membership in N.A.D.H.M. must be made in writing and are subject to the approval of the board of directors. Though membership itself is not necessarily an indication of a company's integrity, it does show their interest in the industry as a whole. For further information, you can contact:

National Association of Dome Home Manufacturers
1701 Lake Avenue
Suite 470
Glenview, Illinois 60025

Contracting with a manufacturer for the purchase of a dome home can mean many different things. Be sure to read all the contracts and literature very carefully. If you're getting a "turnkey" dome home this means that the building will be completed and prepared for occupancy at a prearranged price. The individual elements of the dome are called "components." If the contract just covers components, you can expect to receive only the disassembled pieces—and you may also have to provide interior finishing for the shell yourself.

What can the consumer do to evaluate a manufacturer? Here are some guidelines provided by William Hensel, president of the Domes/ Geodyssey Corporation:

1. Obtain literature from as many component suppliers as possible.
2. Realize that the purchase of the dome shell is the smallest step in erecting a finished house.
3. The purchase of the manufactured components is usually less than 25 percent of the *finished cost* of the dome home.
4. Usable floor space counts. It's the *only* way to evaluate the value of the dome. Diameter is *not* an indication of the floor space or value.
5. Avoid persons or companies using strange math or complicated numbers to describe the dome. Often this simply means that a company is trying to bolster its own credibility rather than inform the public.
6. Know what is supplied—*exactly*!
7. Before you buy anything, take all the literature on your selection to a local contractor and try to pinpoint a finished cost for the complete project from foundation to finish. Then approach a local lending institution with this information.
8. Help from local people is essential. Their reputations keep them in business.
9. Find out what help is supplied with the dome shell. How will your contractor be trained to erect the structure? *How much will it cost?*
10. Find out who pays the freight on the dome home components.

You might also find the following questionnaire helpful. It's the one we used when we started to gather information from dome manufacturers for this book.

1. Company name and address.
2. President's name.
3. Types of domes manufactured.
4. Materials employed in their manufacture.
5. Range of sizes offered. (Diameter and fraction of sphere.)
6. Standard or custom structures? Both?
7. How are your domes offered? (Kit, plans, erected, etc.)
8. Do you do turnkey structures? Is this a standard or custom procedure for you?
9. Do you offer purchasers of your domes a design service? Please elaborate.
10. Have structural analyses been done on your domes? On standards, customs, or both?
11. Do you have an engineering service to do analyses?
12. Would you do an analysis of someone else's dome if requested?
13. What is the price range on your domes? (Typical cost per foot.)
14. How long have you been in business?
15. How many people does your firm employ full-time? Part-time?
16. How many domes have you produced to date?
17. Is there an architect or engineer on your staff? If so, how many of each? (Indicate full- or part-time.)
18. If you have dealers, how many do you have? Generally speaking, where are they concentrated?
19. Are your brochures free? If not, what is the charge?
20. Are there any important new developments not covered in your literature?
21. Do you have F.H.A. or V.A. certification? State, regional, or national?

After you've collected as much information as you can, the next step is to see the finished product and talk with people who have lived in it. A veteran will be able to tell you how well the dome has weathered, how well he likes dome living, and how well he was treated by a particular manufacturer.

Once you've selected a manufacturer, you'll often have to find a contractor with some experience in this specialized field. The company you want to deal with may be in the Midwest, and they may have an efficient crew of subcontractors on hand—but that won't help much if you live in New Jersey.

Be sure to check on shipping rates to your area. Depending on where you live, this cost alone can be considerable. Remember too that in most cases the cost of the commercially produced shell is less than 25 percent of the cost of the completed home. Saving a lot of money shouldn't be your primary concern when considering a commercially prefabricated dome.

With all this in mind, you can use the following list of dome manufacturers to find the one best suited to your needs. Remember, though, that the prices quoted here are all subject to change without notice. You should also remember that the inclusion of professional dome kit and component manufacturers within this book is intended purely as an objective representation. Following the advice presented in other sections of this book, learning as much as you can about domes, and using your common sense, you should be able to make the right choices.

The following directory of major dome home manufacturers is, as far as I know, the only one of its kind. The initial list was compiled from membership information supplied by N.A.D.H.M. There are also a number of manufacturers who aren't affiliated with N.A.D.H.M., and while this isn't necessarily an indication of their professionalism, it does make information-gathering a bit more difficult. I've made every effort to include these independent companies, but it's possible that a few eluded me. So if you're interested in a dome home, it would be a good idea to check around and see if any new companies have started up in your area.

Each listing in the directory is based on information concerning products, services, and corporate structure provided by the manufacturers in response to our questionnaire. The entries were double-checked by the manufacturers and have been approved by them. In some cases, a section in italics follows the corporate listing. This provides comments by Andrew Ralph based on his personal experiences with certain dome home manufacturers. Formerly associated with the Dome East Corporation, Mr. Ralph also contributed to *The Dome Builder's Handbook*.

COMMERCIAL DOME HOME MANUFACTURERS

American Geodesic, Inc.
Freedom Park
2001 Outer Hammond Street
Bangor, Maine 04401

This company has been in business since 1974 and has four full-time employees. They build Omegadome IX, a 2 × 6 wood-panel dome with a half-inch plywood skin. The dome is 32 feet in diameter and 13 feet high, and is a rotated modified ¼3V, built on a 16-foot kneewall. The floor area is 830 square feet, shaped like a triangle with the points cut off for increased use of space near the edges. Shells are available for seven regular domes and three hexagonal domes. Shells for full foundation or pier and pillar foundation come with floor joisting, which is not needed for slab foundation. The costs are about $11 per square foot, erected.

Siding, insulation, doors, windows, and all finishing items are to be added by the purchaser. Blueprints and structural analysis are available to secure a building permit. All shells are fabricated by subcontractors. There are no dealers at this time, but they're being sought; more dome sizes are also being planned. No F.H.A. or V.A. certification yet, but an application is being made. American Geodesic will send you a free flyer; their catalogue is $2.

Omegadome is a dome shell designed in keeping with Fuller's general principles for factory-built housing. It's meant for mass fabrication and fast, easy assembly. It's also been designed to optimize useful living space in a small structure, and the vertical walls make finish carpentry and appliance installation simpler than in a "pure" dome.

The design is an ambitious one, and well geared to the person who must buy and live in a shell. The only fault I can find (more in theory than in use) is that you must use the shell only in the exact shape provided by the manufacturer. This is because of the kneewalls, which are needed to restore the strength lost by cutting away the dome in three places. Even with the added expense of the kneewalls and the mandatory floor joists (so the floor will frame in well every time), Omegadome is quite reasonable in price for the size of dome offered. The well-thought-out design makes it an excellent small dome buy.

The Big Outdoors People
2201 N.E. Kennedy Street
Minneapolis, Minnesota 55413

The Big Outdoors People has been in the dome

business since 1972 and has built about four hundred domes for a variety of uses. They build nine sizes of wood frame-and-skin domes with 2×6, 2×8, or 2×10 frames and ½- or ⅝-inch Blandex (phenolic wood chip) panels. Domes are 15' ⅔, 26' ½, 33' ⁴⁄₉, 33' ⁵⁄₉, 44' ⁵⁄₁₂, 44' ½, 52' ⁷⁄₁₅, 64' and 72'. (The last two diameters are available in several fractions of the sphere.) Special nongeodesic, wood-framed domes with 80 and 100 foot diameters will soon be available. All sizes are available in various stages, from a basic frame-and-skin kit to a shell with interior panels, roofing, insulation, custom windows, a door, and paneled, all-weather, wood foundations.

The Big Outdoors People's all-weather wood foundation system is suited for many soil conditions, but a check with your local building department is essential since some systems are not permissible in certain areas. This foundation consists of studs that are below the grade and sheathed with pressure-treated plywood. The system can be installed regardless of weather conditions and costs less than other foundations.

Custom windows in triangular, circular, or trapezoidal shapes and an integral solar bronze tinting are available for an additional 10 percent over the regular price of each window. Single panes are ¼-inch, heat-tempered glass mounted in neoprene gasketing. The Big Outdoors People's thermal units are two pieces of ³⁄₁₆-inch glass jointed at the edges with a ⅝-inch air space between the two panes. The total thermal window thickness is one inch. Windows are mounted within the exterior panels according to the customer's specific instructions. A five-year guarantee comes with the custom windows, and if any film or dust collects within the space a replacement is provided.

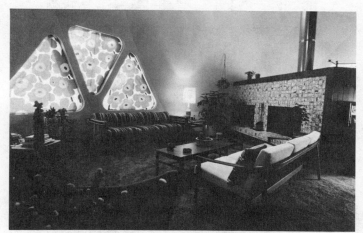

Drafting, consultation, and residential design services are available. The Big Outdoors People's staff will develop plans from customers' ideas and drawings, or the client may pick from one of their standard package plans. If local building officials need structural data, this can also be supplied.

Basic kits range from $2,100 (26' ½) to $8,600 (44' ½), and optional kits range from $3,500 to $25,000. All domes are designed to meet uniform building codes. They have V.A. experimental approval, and an F.H.A. application. Big Outdoors People has a large network of central U.S. dealers, and even some international shipments. Their catalogue is $1.50; a book with fifty pages of floor plans is $5.50. *Dome Flyer*, a quarterly newsletter, is $2.50 for four issues.

This organization is highly conscious of conservation and environmental education and carries a wide

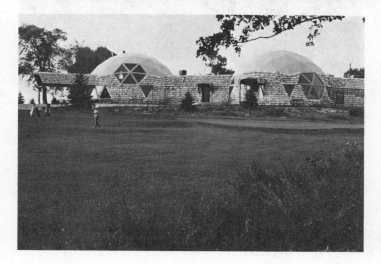

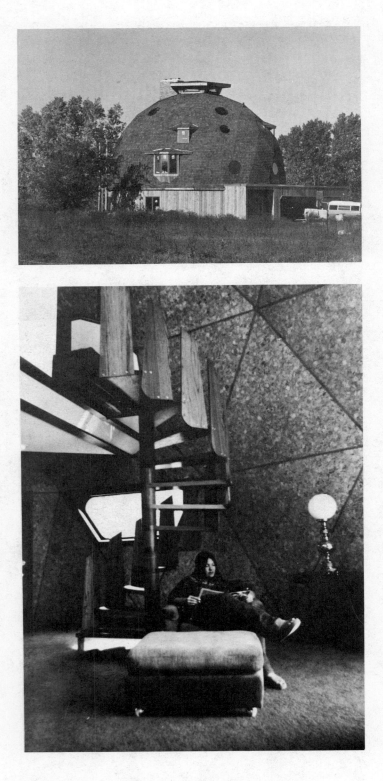

variety of alternative living systems in addition to running a dome home school that covers design and construction as well as mechanical and alternative energy applications. School sessions run for five weeks and are geared for people who either have or are considering buying one of the company's domes—dome-buyers get a discount, and couples get a break too. The Big Outdoors People's dome store carries a slide presentation, model kits, books, wood-burning heaters, water conservation products, solar systems, and wind generators.

The Big Outdoors People domes are designed for both the owner-builder and the contractor. The system does have an advantage for the do-it-yourselfer in that the components are of manageable scale, color coded, and assembly oriented. Many dealers offer "kits" as well as complete turnkey construction services. You can get a good overview of what's involved in building a dome from their cost sheets, showing close construction estimates of a typical dome's cost breakdown as either an owner-builder project or a contractor-built dome. It's very useful planning information and well worth the price of the literature. The shell cost sheet is a fine visual costing tool and is supplemented by cost sheets for windows, roofing materials, etc. I wish more firms had one like it. The system itself seems reasonably simple for a frame-and-skin type dome, and the deep frame gives high insulating quality for a variety of materials.

The hub system developed by The Big Outdoors People is unique. The end plate comes attached to the strut member and is ready for immediate site assembly. The rustproof metals have good tensile strength, and the connection system has been subjected to independent physical and computer analysis. The Big Outdoors People reports that field damage to these members is almost nonexistent, but extra struts are included in case of damage or theft on the site. The frame system alone meets uniform building code loading criteria. The overall pricing is very good for an owner-built dome, and quite acceptable if it's built by a contractor.

Cathedralite Domes
A California Corporation
Box 880
Aptos, California 95003

This company has been in business since 1963 and offers $3/8$, $5/8$, and Pease-type domes with riser walls and/or extensions. These come in 26, 30, 35,

39, 45, 52, and 60 foot diameters in 2 × 4 or 2 × 6 construction. The 2 × 4's and 2 × 6's are clear, select, vertical-grain, kiln-dried #1 Douglas fir; the plywood is CC constructional #1, ½ inch thick. Other materials include standard nails and staples and marine resourcinal glue.

Cathedralite domes are sold in a kit composed of factory-assembled triangles; distributors offer complete construction services. A design service is available on either a custom or stock plan basis. The company prefers that foundation design be done by a local engineer and will do foundation designs only if the client submits a soil analysis and a topographical map. All the domes have been analyzed by hand computations, computer readouts, and field testing by an independent laboratory.

Cathedralite dome home kits use the panel construction system of bolting together a series of triangles to form pentagons and hexagons that in turn form the completed shell. The triangles come in two sizes, one for the pentagons and one for the hexagons. There are sixty triangles in all, forming six pentagons and five hexagons. Five pentagons make up the perimeter of the dome base, the five hexagons are placed above the opening areas connecting two pentagons on either side, and the final pentagon forms the apex.

Complete prices per square foot vary nationwide from $17 to $40; the national average is probably around $25 to $28. The firm has fifty full-time and ten part-time employees and has built over seven thousand domes. It has approximately forty dealers nationwide, with most concentrated in the West, although the company is expanding in the East and Midwest. Their literature includes a free introductory flyer and a more detailed brochure for $3. Cathedralite domes have national F.H.A. and I.C.B.O. approvals, with S.B.C.C. and B.O.C.A. pending.

Creative Structures, Inc.
Box 143
Alto, New Mexico 88312

This company has forty full- and part-time employees. By the summer of 1975, they'd built 25 domes, all by other manufacturers. That year they announced their plans for a new line of domes of their own design. No additional information has been received.

The replies I received from Creative Structures indicated that they were fairly together, but inquiries several months later yielded no reply at all. If you live near them, ask around. . . .

Domes and Homes
Box 176
Roosevelt, New Jersey 08555

This company has sixteen full-time and eight part-time employees. It manufactures eleven sizes of the Pease dome in five diameters with 2 × 4 and plywood construction. Domes range from a 26-foot 2V½ at $6,200 ($12.78 per square foot) to a 59-foot 5V½ at $28,610 ($4.84 per square foot). The regular shell offers red cedar shakes, 1 inch of urethane foam insulation, 16-inch studding, and a basic door, window, and skylight package. Options include doors, windows, skylights, and added insulation. Domes are available in this stage of completion, minus the red cedar shakes, for other roofing systems. Stripped shell kits are also available. Their color brochure is $3.

Domes/Geodyssey Corporation
P.O. Box 206
Amherst, Wisconsin 55406

This company manufactures frame-and-skin dome components: steel connectors, Douglas fir 2 × 6's, and waferboard. The sizes offered are 26', 32'7", 40', and 45', all half spheres. The price range per package is 26'—$3,875; 32'7"—$6,675; 40'—$10,300; 45'—$12,500. The average costs of these domes upon completion (excluding land) may vary in accordance with your own requirements, but a rough estimate would be: 26'—$20,000; 32'7"—$38,000; 40'—$55,000; 45'—$68,000.

Domes/Geodyssey Corporation believes that the owner-builder concept of dome home construction is unrealistic and impractical because building is just too difficult for the average person. Their marketing technique reflects this belief, and their products are sold only to the professional building industry. This protects against owner-builder disasters. Their marketing program trains contractors, designers, architects, and builders, and no service group or contractor builds their first system without supervision.

The geometry of Geodyssey's domes is taken from the Dyna Dome system, but Geodyssey has modified the Dyna Dome hub with rustproof plating, weldments, and new fasteners.

On a recent swing through my neck of the woods, Bill Hensel, President of Domes/Geodyssey, remarked, "What the dome business—if you can call

96

it a business—lacks is a sense of reality." If Hensel has his way, things will soon be very realistic in the little world of domes. He's begun a move to upgrade dome components and is a major force behind N.A.D.H.M.

And what about his own domes? The monolithic Blandex panels Domes/Geodyssey favors eliminate panel creep, but the dome has the inherent limitation of being built only as a hemisphere. The hub system is lined up visually before panel application, a nerve-racking experience for anyone who hasn't done it before. As with all hub systems presently made, firring strips must be applied to the inside of the struts before paneling can be done.

All in all, it's a good contractor-built dome. And if keeping your costs down while having that technical backup for insurance means a lot to you, have your contractor look into Domes/Geodyssey.

Dyna Dome
22226 North 23rd Avenue
Phoenix, Arizona 85027

The Dyna Dome organization headed by Bill Woods occupies a special position among professional dome builders. They're interested in providing a high-quality system at the lowest possible cost, encouraging the owner-builder approach. Bill Woods has been building and supplying people with quality materials and assistance perhaps longer than any other professional in the field. His small organization accounts for the construction of over a thousand domes.

Along with the purchase of a Dyna Dome connector kit, a customer receives an instruction packet that greatly assists in every phase of the construction process, from the pouring of the slab through the finishing of the weather-sealed shell. The instruction packet is about twenty pages long and includes many helpful diagrams illustrating window framing, shingling, cutting the plywood panels, and much more.

Dyna Dome does not supply floor plans. This encourages the owner-builder to use his own ingenuity and talents, and ensures that each dome constructed reflects personal accomplishment. In the event that any problems in construction arise, Bill Woods can always be reached by telephone and will gladly discuss any phase of the process until a suitable solution is reached.

Earth Dynamics, Inc.
Box 1175
Boulder, Colorado 80302

This company has five full-time employees. They've produced about thirty shells and have a 2 × 3 and plywood panel dome in four sizes: 26' 2V½, 39' 3V⅜ and ⅝, and 60' 4V triacon ½. Kits run from $1,995 to $14,500 for basic models. Options include doors, riser walls, windows, and finish kits. A design service is also available.

Earth Dynamics' primary emphasis is on a close client-builder relationship for total house projects. They also do energy consulting and have worked out a solar-heated dome design—one option on the basic dome shell is a 12-inch-deep frame kit allowing enough insulation to give an R-value of over 40. This option makes the dome about 25 percent more expensive than the basic kit. Prices on turnkey houses run in the $17 per square foot range, with typical partially finished 39-foot domes at about $10 per square foot. Individual domes have been approved in Colorado, but no code approval is implied. There are no dealers. For now, Earth Dynamics' literature is free, but a more complete brochure will come out fairly soon, for a modest charge.

Expodome International, Ltd.
1245A Rue St. Nicolas, St. Vincent De Paul
Laval, Quebec H7E 4T7
Canada

This company manufactures flexible-membrane, phenolic-foam-insulated panel, aluminum-skin, inflatable, and transparent insulated domes. The materials employed are clear and reinforced vinyl; aluminum tubing; phenolic foam sandwich panels; stainless hardware; and polycarbonate, acrylic, and aluminum sheeting. It offers 20 to 250 foot circular, rectangular, and elliptical shapes in all fractions of the sphere. Standard and custom structures are also available, as is turnkey service. The company has been in business for five years, with six full-time employees, including one architect and one engineer. There are no dealers in the United States. One Canadian dealer is Seven Islands. Brochures are free.

Geodesic Domes, Inc.
10290 Davison Road
Davison, Michigan 48423

In business for over twenty years, Geodesic

Domes has five full-time and five part-time employees. Figures on the number of domes they've produced were unavailable. Their wood Pease-type domes are built of 2 × 4's and ½-inch plywood and come in the following shapes: 26' 2V½, 30' ⅜ 3V, 45' ⅜ 3V, 39' ⅜ 3V, 39' 3V open canopy, and 60' ½. The basic kits are shells with foundation slab forms. Costs range from $2,800 ($4.63 per square foot) for the 26-foot dome to $19,500 ($5.50 per square foot), based on the ground floor only. Insulation, interior panels, and 24- and 32-inch riser walls are optional, as are extensions and dormers. Geodesic Domes has twenty dealers in the Midwest and South. Their literature is free. Rough cost estimates on houses and blueprints are also available.

In its original form, the Pease shell is good, but it's rather dated and limited compared to others on the market today. If you should want a dome in one of the sizes offered and are capable of seeing a major project through with almost no technical support, a shell from Geodesic Domes is a real sleeper value. But this shell needs a lot of updating to make it the equal of several others now on the market. If your skills are just average, look elsewhere.

Geodesic Homes
Box 1675
Bailey, Colorado 80421

Geodesic Homes has been in business for about five years, but we weren't able to find out anything about the company's internal structure. They make two sizes of 2 × 4 and plywood Pease panel domes: a 26' 2V at $2,595 ($5.19 per square foot) and a 39' 3V ⅜ at $4,895 ($4.45 per square foot). Both shells are offered as basic kits. Options include interior panels, insulation, doors, and windows. No skylights or exterior finish is offered. There is no design service, and there are no dealers. F.H.A., V.A., and I.C. are all claimed, but this may be on a case-by-case basis only. Ask. Brochures are free.

The Hasey Company, Inc.
447 North Main Street
Old Town, Maine 04468

Hasey has been in business for about six years, with 8 to 10 full-time employees. As of spring 1978 they had built 25 domes. Their domes are wood-panel with a plywood skin. Standard domes are available in 24-, 34-, 38-, 48-, and 58-foot diameters sold as shells or finished buildings (the locality may

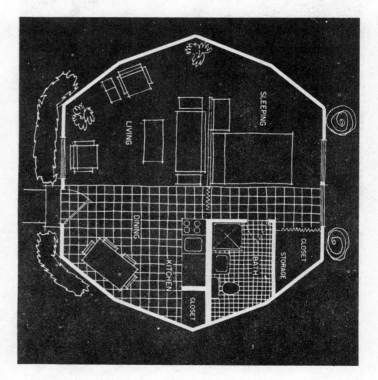

control the amount of finish; turnkey is standard within a 100-mile radius). Bare shell costs range from $2,930 for a 24-foot $\frac{5}{8}$ to $8,590 for a 48-foot $\frac{3}{8}$ dome.

Hasey's design service includes site and spatial planning. Structural analysis is complete on both the 3V dome and the dome in combination with a pressure-treated wood foundation system. The dome has met H.U.D.'s minimum property standards and has received a regional (New England) letter of approval after consideration by H.U.D.'s Technical Suitability of Products Program. There are no dealers. Literature is free, and includes cost estimating charts. Hasey is now working on a dome package for $5 to $10 per square foot.

The Hasey domes are panel domes: $\frac{5}{8}$-inch CDX plywood is used for the exterior paneling, which is nailed and glued, creating a strong system. The panels are held together with $\frac{3}{8}$-inch bolts with $\frac{1}{8}$-inch thick × 1½-inch diameter washers. Coming as a bare shell, the Hasey dome is inexpensive, especially for the insulated versions of the custom shells. If you like both domes and natural wood, this is your dome.

Hexadome of America
Box 2351
La Mesa, California 92041

In business since 1971, this company has produced several hundred domes in California and several thousand in North America for customers who either built from very detailed plans or purchased pre-cut but unassembled color-coded kits. Hexadome is a nongeodesic half dome. The standard diameters are 25 and 32 feet, with larger sizes custom-built. Materials employed are half-inch EX-CDX-1 APA plywood and all-wood 2 × 4's, 4 × 4's, and 4 × 8's. The basic shell kit with no options is $2,500 (about $2.50 a square foot). Turnkey service is available through experienced contractors. Hexadome has dealers and distributors throughout North America. Send a large, stamped, self-addressed envelope for free brochures.

Upon the receipt of a deposit for the Hexadome structure specified, the company will forward 24 × 36 inch full-sized plans with any of the customer's modifications showing extensions, dormers, and the different kinds of foundations used in the construction. These plans are suitable for use in obtaining a building permit, though undoubtedly more data and material will be necessary. The package then delivered will contain the 24 triangular pieces used to construct the hexagonal members and the 3 four-sided pieces, the trapezoids, which are joined to them to make up the completed shell.

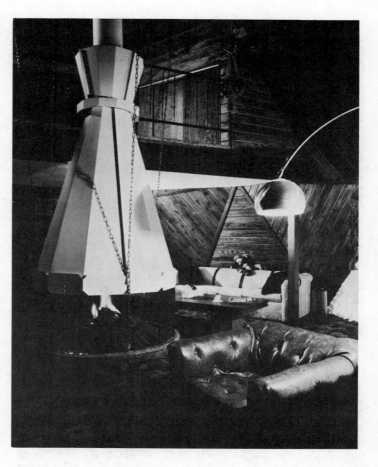

If there is a "Model T" dome around, as panel dome shells go, it has to be either Omegadome IX or Hexadome. I lean slightly toward Hexadome for several reasons: it's more efficient in volume since its 16-foot height permits an upper floor; riser walls can be added to enhance this effect; and the openings can easily be extended out by any carpenter, permitting low-cost expansion of floor space. And the price is right.

Hexadome and Omegadome are both fine examples of thinking a house shell design through in terms of the end product. Hexadome has an edge with its one triangle/one trapezoid components. These hold down factory costs while keeping building methods compatible with conventional carpentry. Both Hexadome and Omegadome are an object lesson in creating something for use from a concept, rather than just hanging doors and windows on a mathematical wonder and calling it the ultimate home. Hexadome is the best basic dome shell to date.

Monterey Domes
P.O. Box 5621-J
Riverside, California 92517

Monterey Domes has been in business since 1970, and builds a 3V icosahedron in diameters of 20, 25, 30, 35, 40, and 45 feet. All are ⅜ or ⅝ spheres using a patented hub construction. The framing members are 2×4, 2×6, and 2×8 Douglas fir and stress-rated Douglas fir plywood. The company makes standard shells, but custom-designed interiors are available. Architectural designers and structural engineers are on the staff. No turnkey is available from the factory, but it can be gotten through dealers. Monterey domes cost between $10 and $45 per square foot; the average owner- builder cost is around $15 a square foot. A fifty-page color catalogue and planning kit is $3, and an assembly manual is available for $5. F.H.A. and V.A. certification are on an individual basis.

Monterey's domes are frame and skin, and the components are covered under a limited ninety-day warranty. All components are color-coded for assembly. The hub devised and patented by Monterey Domes (U.S. Patent #3,990,195) looks like an asterisk or a starfish, and is one solid piece of steel. The flanges extend from a solid center and fit

into presawed slots in the struts. A system of washers, nuts, and bolts holds the strut in place, with two bolts per predrilled strut and hub connection. (The nuts, bolts, washers, and nails are all made of heavy-duty steel, and extras of this hardware are supplied with every Monterey package.) In erecting frame-and-skin domes, it's important that the center of each strut be aligned as exactly as possible with the center point of the hub. This particular system eliminates slip-ups in this area.

The assembly of five hubs and seven struts will result in what Monterey calls a "base tri-triangle," the system of three base triangles that's mounted on the riser wall. Four more base tri-triangles are then completed, mounted on the riser wall, and braced in a vertical position. Completion of the dome frame proceeds in pretty much the same way, merely following the color code. Since construction is not completed until every strut is tightened and in place, it's highly advisable not to walk on the framework.

Monterey Domes has the most beautiful dome brochure I've ever seen. It should be required reading and viewing for the rest of the industry and holds its own in the company of almost any regular house brochure. Monterey Domes makes ingeniously modified straight geodesic domes. They vary in size, are practical and inexpensive (very much so for the size), and can be used as primary dwelling units or as clusters in a series of domes. You should order their brochures and assembly manual just for their information and quality.

Shelter Construction and Development, Ltd.
R.R. #1
Glencairn, Ontario L0M 1K0
Canada

Shelter Construction has been in business since 1969, building wood frame-and-skin domes. The diameters and fractions of spheres are: 15'—¾, 21'4"—¾, 28'6"—½ and ⅝, 35'6"—⅝, 40', 60', 100' (fractions on the last three spheres vary). These are offered in shell kits or designs, either standard or custom. Turnkey is available only to select clients. Full architectural and engineering services, project management services, and design services are available. The engineering service will also provide an analysis. Costs for a stripped kit run from $1,480 to $2,850. Insulation and windows are available, as well as custom domes. The firm has seven full-time and twenty part-time employees, and has made 150 domes. There are no dealers. There's a free information sheet, and a brochure with photos is $2. Most of Shelter Construction's work has been in the Arctic north of 60° latitude.

Space Structures International Corporation (formerly Dome East)
325 Duffy Avenue
Hicksville, New York 11801

In business since 1971, Space Structures has made 134 wooden dome homes and 150 commercial structures. They've built all kinds of structures—geodesics; space frame cylinders; barrel arches; flat roofs; flooring structures; and membrane, panel, and aluminum-skin domes. They manufacture seven sizes of wood frame-and-skin domes in diameters of 30, 39, and 49 feet. All sizes are available as complete shell kits, frame kits, or hub kits. The cost per square foot on structures built by the corporation ranges anywhere from $3.50 to $150. Complete shell kits for their wooden domes range in price from $3,890 to $15,864; frame kits range from $2,430 to $10,633; and hub kits range from $775 to $4,970. Windows and skylights are available, and custom sizes will be built to order. A full design service is available and their brochure is free. The planner package, available for $9.50, contains blank floor plans. Prefabricated panel domes are now available, but they're sold only to clients who show serious interest and motivation. Space Structures International has fifteen dealers or agents in the U.S. and overseas. The firm's staff consists of twenty full-time and ten part-time employees.

Space Structures makes very strong, highly engineered frame-and-skin dome homes. The framing system is built around the hubs, 2 X 4 struts, and sleeves, and is connected with aircraft bolts. It's designed for high winds and snow loads—the frame alone carries the full load of all the shell stresses. Plywood panels or other exterior coverings aren't a factor in the structural integrity of the wood domes, and this allows a greater degree of freedom and flexibility in designing and placing windows and doors.

Formerly known as Dome East, Space Structures has progressed from the days when their focus was mainly dome home manufacturing, and their new corporate name reflects their larger operations. Though still very much a formidable competitor in the dome home marketplace, Space Structures' focus has shifted more toward commercial and industrial structures that demand greater engineering skills, precision, and expertise.

Synapse, Inc.
Box 554
Lander, Wyoming 82520

In business since 1970, with three full-time employees, this company has built twenty-seven domes. They offer ten basic domes from 11'9" to 58'2" in diameter, costing from $1,900 to $17,400 for basic kits. The domes are made of wood panels, 2 X 4's, and plywood, with 24-inch studding standard. Insulation of precut interior panels is also available. Six of these domes are the common five-sided (icosa-based) variety, three use a four-sided (octa) shape, and one is a zome-type building with vertical walls. The four-sided domes can be split in two and expanded in one direction with optional center strips. All are available as custom jobs as well, and some design help can be obtained. There are no dealers. Synapse's brochures are $2. Solar systems are now incorporated in their designs.

Synapse domes are all pre-fab kits based on the bolt-together panel system. The 2 X 4 Douglas fir framing members are spaced 16, 24, or 30 inches apart according to the customer's requirements and then glued and nailed to exterior half-inch plywood that's edge beveled. Weather-proofing and insulation are applied at the Synapse manufacturing plant.

Synapse also manufactures special wing half-panels which may replace triangular component panels, facilitating the installation of rectangular doors. The kits will be shipped anywhere within the continental U.S. and completely erected with interiors anywhere within the Rocky Mountain area. Synapse also sells five 24 X 36 inch blueprints for $75, and interior sheeting diagrams will be furnished upon request. As part of their available options, interior triangular wood paneling can be cut to size. tthey will also make ferrocement domes.

Costs per square foot haven't been listed for Synapse—with the variety of domes available, precise figures would be impossible. In general, the prices run in the $4 to $8.50 per foot range. My compliments to Synapse for designing a nice, overlapping seam system and using gaskets for panel-edge sealing. These shells seem like a good choice for a custom dome. Also worth noting is the fact that Synapse is experimenting with modified dome shapes. Again, benefits for the consumer.

The size of the firm is deceptively small—it's associated with a separate construction firm, Brasel and Sims. This commercial building and highway and structure-contracting company does much of the work on site preparation, foundations, and the ac-

tual building. Synapse, Inc. does only the designing and fabrication of the dome panel kits.

Tension Structures, Inc.
9800 Ann Arbor Road
Plymouth, Michigan 48170

Tension Structures has been in business since 1969 and builds the O'Dome, a 25-foot-diameter half sphere made from twenty fiberglass-urethane foam sandwich panels in an orange peel shape. A solid metal bar is molded into a fiberglass lip at the base that bends inward and is bolted to a platform base. The ironing-board-shaped panels are reinforced by aircraft cable threaded horizontally through each one. At the skylight opening, a metal securing ring holds all the panels in tension. The panels are joined and held together by a tongue-and-groove locking system.

The structure has several code approvals and a class A fire rating. The typical cost per square foot is $18 to $22. Some accessories are available, and the shell comes in four colors or combinations thereof—white, blue, green, and tan. There are dealers and sales agents across the country. Literature is free.

O'Dome is the oldest high-tech dome shell of any kind now begin made for housing. It's a nice unit, but it's of limited use to most owner-builders in the market for their first home because it's just not a basic living unit for most people. It can make a nice maintenance-free vacation cottage, and the plans show ways of adapting the dome to space-increasing foundations. The aesthetics possible with the plastic panels may not appeal to everyone—they range from very slick plastic modern to mild Buck Rogers. But if that appeals to you, feel free. The price is not unreasonable for the unit, but I do protest their giving deceptively low costs per square foot on some units with foundations and decks by adding in an arbitrary one-half of the deck area. The usual and proper practice is to count only the interior living space.

Western Hemisphere, Ltd.
8113 Rush Street
Fort Worth, Texas 76116

Formerly called Xanadu, Ltd., Western Hemisphere Ltd. employs six people. By the summer of 1975, they'd made 32 domes. These are 39-foot 3V 3/8 and 5/8 geodesic domes with panels made of a fiberglass plasticized honeycomb filled with ver-

milite. Doors and windows are optional. No retail costs are given, but dealer costs indicate that the retail price should be reasonable. Shipping will be cheap, since a 3/8 dome only weighs about 3,000 pounds.

When erected, the dome is weatherproof with no additional work. The manufacturer claims the dome will have a twenty-five-year life until the roof needs a repaint. Their dome shells have been analyzed, and a design service is available. A cement-fiberglass hybrid panel dome is being developed.

There have been individual F.H.A. approvals, but there won't be code approval for the dome until H.U.D. and other government agencies get a definition of what goes on with plastics as building components. The dome *does* carry the same fire rating as a metal building. Western Hemisphere has fourteen dealers; their literature is free.

Along with Tension Structures' O'Dome, Western Hemisphere's Manana Dome is among the first of a new kind of panel dome that will use structural materials other than wood. These domes will have monolithic panels that will result in stronger, more flexible, and maintenance-free dome shells of all kinds. They should be relatively cheap, too, since these other materials are far better suited than wood to factory-produced housing.

I have no experience with this dome, but am fascinated with the concept. The government has financed a few—the old D.E.W. line radomes are an indication of how they should hold up. They lasted well in the Arctic and have had to be taken down, now that they're obsolete, to avoid littering the landscape. And they date from a fairly primitive era of fiberglass technology. I suspect that you'll find they're fine. The upcoming fiberglass cement dome sounds like a real winner—cheap, strong, and maintenance free. The existing dome is not expensive either, because it's fairly complete after erection. It should be quite a dome.

The following builders, contractors, designers, and architects all have had experience with low cost, energy-efficient dwellings. Should you need assistance or have questions in these areas, contact the appropriate person or firm.

American Dome Company
1026 Sunset Trail
Webster, New York 14850

The American Dome Company serves as a

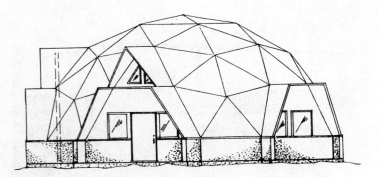

DOME BUILDING CONSULTANTS

source of information for people interested in dome homes and functions as a counseling organization, assisting individuals in their selection of products, planning, and building procedures. The company will forward information to people within the dome industry via a bimonthly newsletter that reflects the consumer's interests and needs. The company hopes to expand their publication into a monthly general-circulation magazine.

Burt Hill Kosar Rittelman Associates
400 Morgan Center,
Butler, Pennsylvania 16001

Their services include programming, feasibility and energy studies, design, construction details and specifications, construction management, research and development, proposal preparation, writing, and consultation. In addition, a full range of consultation services can be tailored to any particular individual's needs. They charge hourly fees for personal office visits to discuss conservation on existing homes and energy conservation potential on builders' homes. A full range of percentage design or architectural fees are also offered.

Burt Hill Kosar Rittelman Associates feels the most important service they can offer is to help people choose the proper methods to conserve nonrenewable resources and to produce or use renewable income energy resources such as wind and solar power.

Steve Coffel
P. O. Box 507
Darby, Montana 59829

Steve Coffel's services mainly involve consulting, underground building, and passive solar design techniques.

Howard Johnson
Domaine
Box 55
Mt. Desert Island, Maine 04660

Working along the lines of the custom builders presented in the next chapter, Howard Johnson is concerned with providing his clients with an environment that is affordable, practical, and functional. He favors Bill Woods' Dyna Dome connector system, and used it in constructing his own home. Prospective clients should be familiar with the dome project because Howard Johnson is a selective builder who bases his decisions on the client's exhibited degree of interest in a dome home.

Charles Simms
19 Harrison Street
New York, New York 10013

Charles Simms works extensively with architect Robert Godwin. Services include general contracting, project management, and several subcontractor services. He also offers original design, drafting room, and consultation services.

Alex Wade
Station Road
Barrytown, New York 12507

Alex Wade is an architect and coauthor of *Thirty Energy Efficient Houses.*

Zomeworks Corporation
P. O. Box 712
Albuquerque, New Mexico 87103

Zomeworks is a highly innovative firm founded by Steve Baer, a pioneer in solar energy research and design. Steve Baer's books include *Zome Primer, Dome Cookbook* (now out of print), and *Sunspots.*

Spirex Structures, Inc.
21750 Schmeman
Warren, Michigan 48089

The principal ingredient in these domes is styrofoam. Their literature states that although the plastic foam contains a fire retardant, once ignited it can burn very rapidly, producing dense smoke. These large domes seem better suited to commercial use, but Spirex's Stephen J. Waling tells me their domes can be adapted for residential use.

Spirex has built about two hundred domes using their own spiral generation technique, a construction method in which nine-foot slabs are laminated on top of one another in a circular pattern until the dome is completed. The open eye that remains at the top is then filled with a prefabricated section— any vents or skylights required at the eye are built into this final section, which is cemented in last to ensure structural stability.

The domes rest on a block foundation, and a tension ring of steel or reinforced concrete is applied around the circumference of this base. The tension ring starter strip is mechanically fastened, the spiral generation equipment is put in place, and then the dome-building process begins. One of the most im-

INDUSTRIAL AND COMMERCIAL MANUFACTURERS

portant parts of the construction equipment is the fusion head—this transmits steel wire so that the foam blocks are reinforced at every laminated surface. The fusion head is controlled by a sensing device to ensure precision.

The welded steel wire on the dome surface is held in place with roofing nails, and the outside of the shell is protected with a thin layer of mortar. This mortar, modified with a latex additive, is sprayed in layers with a maximum thickness of half an inch. The final layer is a white, textured coat something like everyday stucco, with a thickness of between an eighth and a quarter of an inch. The inside of the foam shell can be coated with plaster or other coverings if necessary.

Temcor
2825 Toledo Street
Torrance, California 90503

Before kit companies came into being and before people were again thinking about the dome as a family dwelling space, huge commercial domes were being built by a few well-established corporations. Under Temcor's supervision, one such dome was erected at the South Pole by Navy Seabees for a project known as "Operation Deep Freeze." Sixty-five hundred components were shipped sixteen thousand miles to complete a structure that housed three buildings for the National Science Foundation's polar research project.

Temcor's gigantic domes are made of heat-treated anodized structural aluminum and are virtually maintenance-free. They weigh about 2½ pounds per square foot, have withstood 40 pounds per square foot of snow and 125-mile-per-hour winds, and are noncombustible and earthquake resistant. Temcor also makes domes of transparent and translucent acrylic affixed to an aluminum alloy framework.

These multifaceted, highly subdivided gold- or silver-colored structures were probably among the first domes many of us ever saw. Although manufacturers like Temcor are not geared toward the housing industry, their precision and the very appearance of their domes have been a factor in the acceptance of domes as a possible dwelling alternative. They *do* make beautiful domes, but please don't write to them just out of curiosity.

Triodetic Structures Limited
335 Roosevelt Avenue
Ottawa, Ontario, K2A 1Z2
Canada

Triodetic Structures uses mill-finished or anodized aluminum or stainless steel for their space-frame and latticed shells. Galvanized steel is used for other large projects such as warehouses or factories because it eliminates the need for any further protective finishes and maintenance. Triodetic Structures' covering systems include simple fabric, plywood with a weathering membrane and urethane foam, insulated and noninsulated metal sheeting, and wood paneling.

Triodetic Structures has been in business over fifteen years and has built 1000 to 1500 structures, mostly for commercial, institutional, and industrial use. The company's domes can be used for home building, but all their products have a commercial orientation. A rule of thumb: if you aren't spending $100,000 and you don't like metal domes, these domes aren't for you. But they *are* very beautiful.

Triodetic Structures has built *some* noncommercial domes, one of which is in the Bahamas. The dome is a two-story structure with a thirty-foot-diameter section cut out and raised to provide for windows. The floor of the upper level was created by suspending an inverted duplicate of the raised thirty-foot-diameter section. The building is supported by twelve legs that are independent of the door frames. Triangular laminated wood panels were used to cover the dome, and they were attached directly to the aluminum tube struts. Aluminum shingles for the exterior were laid down over a layer of felt.

With the assistance of one supervisor, the construction was carried out by local laborers. No heavy equipment was used, and the main dome was put together on the ground. It was lifted into position by hand, using the roof panels as supports. The covering and windows were in place within sixty days.

Unadilla Silo Company, Inc.
Unadilla, New York 13849

The growing acceptance of the dome has helped popularize other architectural dwelling forms. Unconventional dwellings seem to be more and more common, although they're usually spawned by either an overabundance or a severe lack of money. It's cheaper to convert than it is to tear down, and with the discovery that the form of a building need

not always dictate its function, all sorts of doors open to imaginative living situations. Why not live in a converted barn or church, especially if it's fun and works well?

Unadilla Silos has been in business since 1906, and has been building laminated rafters since 1958. They've supplied rafter components for a variety of unconventional structures in addition to their main silo and arch-roof barn business. They employ a large number of people and have about three hundred dealers or agents throughout the Northeast; these are mostly farm supply firms. Preliminary information is free, but there's a charge for dome elevations.

The curved arches manufactured by Unadilla Silo are made of Douglas fir laminated with waterproof glue. They work very well in an A-frame since the curved arches provide more headroom than the straight members used in typical A-frames. And second-story floor space is also greater because of these arches.

Silo houses and modified A-frames are a relatively new development for the Unadilla people, as are the custom domes that architects have designed from Unadilla's laminated rafters. The company corresponds willingly and has a lot of fun with whatever they're doing—in a letter to us they refer to Steve Badanes, who designed the helix and helmet domes built with their products, as the "Jersey Devil."

Unadilla Silo is one of those lucky discoveries you come across when you're researching an area: they build a nearly universal laminated wood arch, with quality, strength, and a modest price tag. Architects have used it to spec out four domes: two plain, segmented domes; a "helmet" dome for a hillside with an unusual multilevel living pattern; and a helix dome that uses several sizes of arches to create a growth spiral like a seashell—the one exterior view that I've seen is both striking and very organic, to use an overworked word accurately. The latter two domes are the work of Steve Badanes, a very gifted and creative guy.

I recommend Unadilla's products for two reasons: their silo houses are a nice fantasy tool and blend nicely with domes, and their arches provide an affordable way for an architect (or any other competent person) to design a truly unique dome.

Fabrico Manufacturing Corp., 1300 W. Exchange Ave., Chicago, Illinois 60609

Chapter 6. Custom Dome Building

Envirotecture
134 North Ojai Street
Santa Paula, California 93060

Dome West
181 Pier Avenue
Santa Monica, California 90405

Dyna Dome
22226 North 23rd Avenue
Phoenix, Arizona 85027
(See entry in Chapter V)

Beyond the mainstream of professional dome builders and corporate manufacturers, there are a few custom builders who operate on a more personal level. Custom builders should not be considered dome building specialists; it's more accurate to describe them as highly skilled professionals who happen to build some domes. These builders are concerned about the impact our dwellings have on our everyday lives, and you in turn will have to think seriously about your personal environment before asking them to design and build a living space to suit your needs.

Custom building organizations like Envirotecture and Dome West are definitely not in competition with dome kit manufacturers. While manufacturers are geared toward a level of building accessible to a large number of people, custom builders are capable of specializing. The two groups also work in different ways. In order for dome kit manufacturers to perfect their products a cooperative effort is necessary, but a sharing of industrially applicable ideas isn't a profitable venture under the free enterprise system. Manufacturers are encouraged to pro-

tect their knowledge and develop sets of standards and designs that distinguish them from the competition. Financially speaking, producing a very different product can be as advantageous as producing a better one.

Though the general trend is toward an upgrading of commercially produced products, a kit manufacturer's business is based on the production of standardized components, and a constant flow of innovative changes defeats the purpose of standardization. So it stands to reason that some kit manufacturers are better off refining the systems they're presently using, most of which are patented and protected to the fullest extent of the law.

Economy in shipping is another problem, but if materials are available in your area this can be handled admirably. The saving in shipping costs is one inherent advantage in purchasing only connector kits, since all other materials are bought locally. Construction of the kits, unless the manufacturer provides turnkey service, can of course be another matter.

On the other hand, construction is quite naturally the custom builder's forte. The same man who sits behind a desk drafting, designing, and computing structural analyses often loves nothing better than to work on the buildings he's designed, getting right down to the sore thumbs, sweat, and dirt that building a home is all about. The heart of the custom builder's business lies in craftsmanship and personal talent, not standardized design. The quality of the construction overshadows the importance of structural and technical innovation, and both the client's needs and the custom builders' styles are unique. Custom builders are also more apt to use traditional materials. Wood, glass, stone, and rock will be combined, often achieving a sensitive blend of new and old.

Approaching the custom builder is not quite the same as approaching a manufacturer. There are no prearranged plans. Everything will have to be discussed and worked out, and the client should be receptive and cooperative. Many people are still drawn to the dome project by the prospect of great financial savings, but it often turns out that even kit projects can easily cost as much as $35 a square foot. Obviously, cutting corners is not the motivation a custom builder looks for in a client interested in a dome.

Custom builders often prefer smaller domes because a dome that's too expansive just doesn't have the same effect as a smaller one. And larger domes are harder to heat and cool.

In a custom-built dome, shorter struts are also featured. These form smaller triangles to establish an ideal relationship between plane and curvature, emphasizing the circular quality of the dome. When struts are long, the triangles become very large, creating a few very large, flat facets that break up the circular effect inherent in the dome.

Longer struts and larger components facets are used in some kits because this facilitates the installation of more conventional doors and windows, and these are easier to install and easier to seal against moisture and air penetration. Expansion and contraction don't affect them as much as triangular windows and doors, which are always tricky. But triangular elements are an integral part of a dome, and breaking up the pattern results in a loss of the overall effect.

In designing a dome for a family or a large group of people, a custom builder is apt to suggest *several* smaller domes as opposed to one large-scale building. This allows more privacy, and the small domes can be used as separate rooms.

Cluster formations also provide variety. The functions of different rooms can be switched from time to time, changing the view as well as the movement and flow throughout the dwelling. Any variety is a stimulant and deters the boredom of day-to-day repetitive patterns. Variety can also be incorporated into cluster formations by building different-sized domes or using different materials—light wood in one dome, dark in another, and a combination of the two in yet another.

The land you're building on will also be an important consideration for the custom builder. For exam-

ple, the site of the Goldberg-Saltzman property shown in the color section is surrounded by tall eucalyptus trees. The egg-shaped elliptical dome blends in with them perfectly. But in a desert environment a different approach is necessary. Desert domes built by Envirotecture are always sunk about four feet underground. This helps to regulate the interior climate and brings the visual plane down nearer to the horizon, the focal point for desert environments. The dome doesn't extend so far above ground, and this provides a more pleasing exterior view.

Understandably, a custom builder is often confronted with challenges and demands that lean more toward the abstract. Consider the needs of the Krishnamurti Foundation in their Ojai Valley, California schoolhouse—the creation of a timeless structure with an interior in which a person tends to lose a sense of self.

The site for the school is a 150-acre lot below the Topa Topa mountains amid a thicket of oak trees. The project covers 1,200 square feet, cost about $170,000, and was designed and constructed by Carey Smoot of Envirotecture and his specially selected crew. A harmonious blending of the struc-

ture and grounds makes a full view of the facility impossible from any angle. In the three-building complex, the main structure is composed of three hexagons joined to form a single open room in which movable screens provide interior division. The other two buildings are a workshop/crafts center and a storage space with washrooms.

The main building looks larger than it is because of the high ceiling supported by large wooden columns. Usually such columns would be made from laminated stock, but these are all solid wood and had to be turned on a special lathe. They were then left to check and crack as they dried, a natural aging process that gives the feeling of tree trunks within the structure. Skylights filter sunshine into the room, and the movement of the sun highlights the wood columns, the floor, and the carved wooden doors and window sashes.

The luxuriousness of the building is not distinct and definable; it's the result of many interrelated subtleties. The exterior siding, for example, is a relatively inexpensive knotty pine that's been left to weather. As time passes, its color and texture will blend with those of the surrounding oak trees. Copper nails were used to fasten the siding; gradually they'll bleed green against the weathering gray sur-

face, a graceful way of aging. Unlike steel nails, copper nails won't rust out and snap, and the heads won't pop off as time passes. Solid copper flashing was also used, again with endurance in mind.

The roof of the Krishnamurti structure, constructed by Norman Siefert, is a work of art in itself. It resembles a rippling lake surface, changing in appearance as sunlight is reflected from different angles. During heavy rains, water pours off the roof in a carefully channeled pattern. Because of the many merging bends and curves, each shingle had to be cut by hand in a trapezoidal shape. The red cedar shingles were pressure treated with fire retardant and secured by copper nails. Each shingle was steamed and nailed in place while it was still hot and pliable.

Handcrafted structures like the Krishnamurti school and the Saltzman-Goldberg dome are surely not answers to major housing problems on a grand scale, but they do serve as examples of what can be accomplished through a sensitive approach to the ideal dwelling. Not enough work has been done in environmental psychology to establish exactly how an individual or family will be affected by a certain type of structure or a particular design, but there is some information available that we can consider

when we make decisions about our personal environment.

The custom-built house reflects its owner's aspirations, personality, and self-image. Whether we're aware of it or not, our houses are projections of ourselves, and the fact that one day we finally start working with wood, hammer, and nails doesn't mean we haven't been mentally building our homes since we were children. Actually, by the time we're adults and are ready to get started with building, financing, and the other aspects of providing ourselves with a home, quite a bit of planning and preliminary investigation has already taken place.

A custom builder will want to become familiar with your ideal dwelling and learn more about your lifestyle and aspirations. The right building for you will grow out of this dialogue, and, if everything works well, it can become almost a symbol of your way of life.

For centuries architecture was a primary means of expression, one of the richest ways of communicating human aspirations, desires, and capabilities. Sensitive custom builders continue this tradition and are aware of the symbols and signs that can add richness to daily life. They recognize the

Norman Siefert completing the roof of the Krishnamurti center.

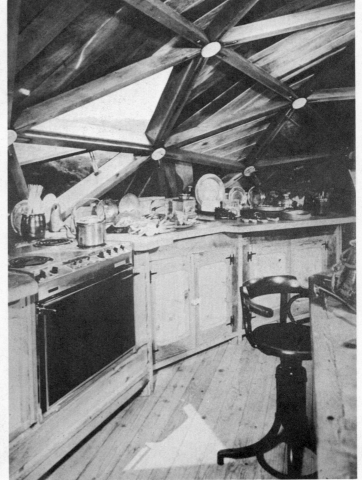

way certain shapes relate to our feelings about ourselves and use the basic building forms—the circle, the triangle, the square, and the cross—to express these feelings.

Once these common patterns held a deeper meaning. Today we usually see their shapes only as something pleasing to the eye, and our loss of perception shows in our dwellings. As appreciation fades, so does the need for expressive and enriching living space. And when regard for the building is low, we're left with flimsiness. A sense of excitement and personal involvement has been lost, and it won't be regained until we have a better understanding of what living space involves.

The custom builder must be knowledgeable about space and the effects of closure. Custom domes are expensive, but their redeeming value lies in the extraordinary quality of space that can be achieved. Any dwelling that's constructed with loving care—dome or nondome—will reflect that care, but a dome designed and built especially for you can impart an exceptional feel that's immediately noticeable the minute you enter the building.

Most of us are familiar with the difference in the way a room "feels" when thriving plants are added.

We know that different people's dwellings can have completely different atmospheres. Sometimes we can isolate particulars that we think are responsible for our reactions to different kinds of space, but we still don't know all that much about how our dwellings will affect us as people. We only know that their impact is very strong and affects our lives every day.

What subtle discomforts and debilitating circumstances might we now be experiencing and completely failing to notice? The body reacts physiologically to situations of pleasure, stress, and strain—poor design and irritating conditions can sometimes quite literally induce mental illness.

Poorly designed housing projects have had disastrous effects. At the Pruitt-Igoe housing project in St. Louis, there was very little privacy, and many irritated young people left their apartments. Their living conditions were unbearable, so they tended to gather in communal areas which inevitably turned into battlegrounds. Upon its construction in the 1950s, the project had been highly acclaimed. Less than twenty years later, it was partially demolished because of the hazards it presented its few remaining occupants.

But the reverse is also true. Architectural design

119

can prove very beneficial. In a hospital in Saskatchewan, rooms and corridors for a schizophrenic ward were designed in varying patterns of trapezoids and parallelograms. Many patients recovered more rapidly than expected because they were forced to use long-dormant thought processes in adapting to a varied environment.

It's important to think about all this when designing your dome, but don't get carried away. As in any other form of dwelling design, it's a good idea to leave your plans open to a bit of flexibility. Too much planning has a tendency to lock the inhabitants into set patterns and situations before the environment has had a chance to be tested. It may also be a response to a present situation that may vanish or change with the new dwelling. New circumstances may stimulate new needs, and there's little that can be done to anticipate these new needs. A strictly defined system may be difficult to alter, causing new and possibly even more frustrating conditions.

If you let it, a home can have a tendency to plan itself. Sleeping, eating, and living areas may just evolve. Sometimes when homes have been "overdesigned," the occupants end up disliking what were thought to be its positive aspects and loving the "mistakes."

Bibliography

HISTORY OF THE DOME

Buckminster Fuller at Home in the Universe, by Alden Hatch. Crown Publishers, 1 Park Ave., N.Y., N.Y. 10016 (1974). 279 pp., $7.95. Paperback: Dell Books, 245 East 47th St., N.Y., N.Y. (1976), $3.25

This biography of Fuller was written by a lifelong friend. It's an interesting and warm account, focusing not on Fuller's scientific and technical accomplishments but on the man himself. An intimate biography and a stirring account of Fuller—an ingenious, provocative, and very human figure.

Developments in Structural Form, by Rowland J. Mainstone. M.I.T. Press, 28 Carleton St., Cambridge, Mass. 02142 (1975), 350 pp. $25.

Mainstone examines all the elementary building forms—domes, arches, beams, etc.—tracing their development chronologically and emphasizing the problems designers have had confronting them. His discussions of structural technology, and man's use of materials make the evolution of building and architectural design seem as natural as the evolution of any living species. The book is comprehensive, understandable, and well written. It contains over three hundred photographs and drawings, most of them by the author.

The Dome, by E. B. Smith. Princeton University Press, Princeton, N. J. 08540 (1950, reprint 1971). 228 pp.

This scholarly book traces the development of dome symbolism and the evolution of the dome as a structure. An extraordinarily ambitious volume. Smith proves that the dome was primarily a housing form that gradually acquired imaginative values which were later expressed in permanent, monumental domes. Well researched and well written, the book is comprehensive and fascinating.

Ideas and Integrities, by Buckminster Fuller. Collier Books, 866 Third Ave., N.Y., N.Y. (1969). 319 pp. $2.95.

This book gives a broad overview of Fuller's thoughts and ideas. It's extraordinarily complex and technical, and packed with information. To most of us, it's astounding and at times baffling to see the way Fuller's mind works, but the book is certainly a tribute to his cerebral capabilities. It's difficult to read, but worth the effort since it contains scientific, historical, and architectural material plus much, much more.

Roman Architecture and Its Principles of Construction Under the Empire, by G.T. Rivoira. The Clarendon Press, 200 Madison Ave., N.Y., N.Y. 10016 (1925). 310 pp. $50. Reprint: Hacker Art Books, 54 W. 57th St., N.Y., N.Y. 10019 (1972).

A difficult book to find. Rivoira provides a 32-page appendix on the evolution of the dome up to the seventeenth century. He also gives an account of the methods used in the construction of many of the world's most famous domes. The book contains many interesting photographs, including one of Michelangelo's model for the dome of St. Peter's.

ARCHITECTURE AND LIVING SPACE

Form Follows Fiasco, by Peter Blake. Little, Brown and Company, 34 Beacon St., Boston, Mass. 02106 (1974). 169 pp. $6.95.

An indictment of the modern architectural movement by a well-known architectural critic and fourth-generation modern architect. This book explains in discomforting detail the failures of modern architecture. A dynamic and fascinating revelation of the power that architecture and architects wield over individuals and cultures throughout the world. The book is neither technical nor academic, rather it is geared toward the wide readership that it certainly deserves.

The Hidden Dimension, by Edward T. Hall. Doubleday & Company, 245 Park Ave., N.Y., N.Y. 10017 (1966). 201 pp. Paperback: $2.50.

This book provides a greater awareness of man's use of space in terms of both the distance between two beings and as a means of expression. The author, an anthropologist, presents an enlightening discussion of environmental influences on the conscious and unconscious mind. Highly informative, interesting, and well-written, this book along with another of Hall's works, *The Silent Language,* is among the handful of books that have been written in a highly neglected, yet extremely important field.

123

Nonverbal Communication in Architectural Form and Functions, by Rikki Smoot (1977). Mimeographed. 15 pp. Copies available upon request: Rikki Smoot, c/o Envirotecture, 134 N. Ojai St., Santa Paula, Ca. 93060.

This unpublished report describes the relationship between various architectural forms and their respective cultures, including an analysis of psychological projections as represented by the choice of personal dwelling space. Ms. Smoot also deals with the influences of spatial arrangements on social and personal well-being. Well researched and thoroughly documented, the report contains a complete and up-to-date listing of resources available on the topic.

Psychology of the House, by Olivier Marc. Thames and Hudson, 30–34 Bloomsbury St., London WC1B 3QP, England (1977). 144 pp. $12.95.

An extraordinarily interesting book written by a man who is both an architect and an analyst, *Psychology of the House* should be read in conjunction with *Form Follows Fiasco*. A well-written work based on years of research and experience within two seemingly unrelated fields. Mr. Marc sees our homes and our use of architectural space as keys to a greater understanding of ourselves. He provides a wealth of information, photographs, and illustrations.

Shelter, edited by Lloyd Kahn. Shelter Publications, P.O. Box 279, Bolinas, Ca. 94924 (1973). 176 pp. $6.

Shelter is a marvelous collection of handmade dwelling ideas from all over the world. Since its metamorphosis from the nonprofit Pacific Domes Company into a nonprofit, educational publishing organization, Shelter Publications has broadened and enriched its horizons, producing the finest volume of handcrafted shelter ideas available. This book will probably stand as the most exhaustive compilation of its kind—at least until the publication of *Shelter 2*. A must for the owner-builder.

DOME BUILDING

The Dome Builder's Handbook, edited by John Prenis. Running Press, 38 S. 19th St., Phila., Pa. 19103 (1973). 107 pp. $4.

A sourcebook of interesting thoughts and ideas. Though its orientation is not geared toward what most would consider permanent residential dwelling, it serves as a valuable reference tool and an aid in building a variety of domes. Contains useful math and model-building information.

Dome Notes, by Peter Hjersman. Erewhon Press, P.O. Box 4253, Berkeley, Ca. 94704 (1975). 202 pp. $7.50.

A very comprehensive work leaning more toward the mathematical and technical aspects of dome building. Mr. Hjersman covers everything from models, tensegrities, fire testing, and hub testing to playground and alternative structures. *Dome Notes* contains nearly three hundred ink drawings plus an extensive bibliography that should form the core of a serious dome builder's library.

Domebooks 1 & 2, edited by Lloyd Kahn. Shelter Publications, P.O. Box 279, Bolinas, Ca. 94924.

Domebook 2 has been taken out of print because, after years of living in and building domes, the people involved in publishing the book have become disillusioned with them. The book is still available in libraries and contains information on geodesic geometry and chord factors, as well as models that may prove valuable for reference purposes. However, it should definitely not be thought of as a guide to building permanent dwellings. It is a compilation of the ideas and experiences of dome builders from the late '60s and early '70s and is reflective of both the idealism and the conflicting interests of the times.

GENERAL BUILDING TECHNIQUES

All Your Home Building and Remodeling Questions Answered, by Stanley Schuler. The Macmillan Company, 866 Third Ave., N.Y., N.Y. 10022 (1971). 524 pp. $9.95.

A question-and-answer book that covers land, planning, money, contractors, construction, and much more. A nice reference tool to have on hand.

Basic Carpentry by John Capotosto. Reston Publishing Company, 11480 Sunset Hills Rd., Reston, Va. 22090 (1977). 525 pp. Paperback: $6.95.

A book that goes far beyond basic carpentry. Mr. Capotosto covers scaffolding construction, foundations, windows, chimneys, fireplaces, and more. The book is sequentially arranged to parallel the process of house construction and is intended for students who wish to learn carpentry in order to become professionals. This is a comprehensive text well worth the price.

Do-It-Yourself House-Building Step-By-Step, by Charles D. Neal. The Macmillan Company, 866 Third Ave., N.Y., N.Y. 10022 (1973). 246 pp. $12.

Offers an explanation of how to plan, construct, and finish a house. Mr. Neal discusses a single procedure for every step of the house-building process. The book illustrates the construction of three different houses and is a complete guide to all phases of the building process from foundation to finish.

Energybooks 1 & 2, edited by John Prenis. 38 S. 19th St., Phila., Pa. 19103 (1975, 1977). 112 pp., $4; 128 pp., $5.

These two collections of information on all kinds of alternate sources of energy are of interest to both the layman and the backyard experimenter. Among the many topics discussed are wind and solar energy and methane, plant, and trash power.

The Handmade Greenhouse From Windowsill to Backyard, by Richard Nicholls. Running Press, 38 S. 19th St., Phila., Pa. 19103 (1975). 128 pp. $4.95.

An extensive guide to greenhouse construction for beginning and experienced builders on a variety of budgets. Includes step-by-step illustrated plans for a dome greenhouse with various options. Clear, accurate, and very well written.

The Higson Home Builder's Guide, by James D. Higson. Nash Publishing, 1 DuPont St., Plainview, N.Y. 11803 (1972). Paperback: 359 pp. $7. Craftsman revised edition: 1977.

This book, written by a southern California builder and designer, doesn't deal with the physical construction of a house; instead it familiarizes the reader with the various steps involved in building any residential dwelling. Includes charts and illustrations, plus a breakdown of construction costs, schedules, and hardware.

The Loft Book, by Jim Wilson. Running Press, 38 S. 19th St., Phila., Pa. 19103 (1975). 96 pp. $6.95.

Design, construction, and finishing ideas that apply not only to lofts but to all areas with limited space. Highly informative, practical, and enjoyable. Full color illustrations.

Low-Cost, Energy-Efficient Shelter for the Owner and Builder, edited by Eugene Eccli. Rodale Press, 33 E. Minor St., Emmaus, Pa. 18049 (1976). $5.95.

The title of this book exactly describes its contents. Mr. Eccli presents practical ideas and building plans to assist the owner-builder in the construction of comfortable, low-cost homes.

The Owner-Built Home, by Ken Kern. Scribners, 597 Fifth Ave., N.Y., N.Y. 10017 (1975). $12.95. Paperback: $6.95.

This book is required reading for anyone thinking about building their own home. Filled with tried and tested practical ideas gained through years of experience as a master builder and craftsman. Also includes many other ideas that are worth knowing about. This is well-written and comprehensive, and takes into account many of the more sensitive aspects of home building so often neglected by those less talented and experienced than Mr. Kern.

The Shelf Book, by Jon M. Zegel. Running Press, 38 S. 19th St., Phila., Pa. 19103 (1977). 128 pp. $4.95.

Gives the necessary information to solve shelving needs. *The Shelf Book* begins with the basics and goes on to provide step-by-step drawings illustrating various construction techniques. Well written, clear, and comprehensive, the book supplies many new ideas, including hanging shelves that work very well in domes.

Shop Tactics, by William Abler. Running Press, 38 S. 19th St., Phila., Pa. 19103 (1976). 128 pp. $3.95.

Any home owner or builder will learn a lot from Mr. Abler's book, which deals with all kinds of building materials as well as tools, molds, and measurement.

The Skylight Book, by Al Burns. Running Press, 38 S. 19th St., Phila., Pa. 19103 (1976). 112 pp. $4.95.

The first and only book devoted completely to

skylights. A thorough step-by-step manual filled with diagrams, photographs, and clear instructions that will enable anyone reasonably handy to build his own skylights—skylights that won't leak. Geodesic skylight designs included.

Your Engineered House, by Rex Roberts. M. Evans and Company, 216 E. 49th St., N.Y., N.Y. 10017 (1974). 237 pp. Paperback: $4.95.

Mr. Roberts' popular book contains valuable information on building sites, planning, and design, as well as building tips and techniques. Despite the fact that other experts have questioned Roberts' framing and insulation suggestions, his book remains a useful reference tool. The writing is clear, and the material is presented in a friendly, informal manner.